POWER BIBLE

GUIDEBOOK

An Introduction to Reading the Bible

Green Egg Media

Table of Contents

Chapter 1: Exploring the Bible

Chapter 2: Connecting the Old and New Testaments

Chapter 3: The Temple and the Festivals

Chapter 4: Life and Times of the Bible

Chapter 1

Exploring the Bible

In the beginning, God created our beautiful world and made human beings in His own image. But the people turned away from God, rejected His love, and chose to live their own way. The world was dark and full of sin, but God had a plan. He promised that a messiah would come through the nation of Israel. He would be the Savior of the world, defeating sin and evil and making a way for a restored relationship between God and the people He created.

The Bible is more than a history book. It is a holy book, inspired by God. The story unfolds across 66 books and over 1,600 years, revealing God and His plan of salvation: that a sinful people can be forgiven and live with Him forever.

1. What Kind of Book Is the Bible?

Many Books Within One

The Bible is one big book containing 66 different books, written during different periods of time. These 66 books are arranged in a special order. The Old Testament focuses on God's promise of salvation and on the coming of Jesus Christ. The New Testament explains the fulfillment of that promise through the gospel of Jesus Christ.

The Old Testament contains 39 books, covering the beginning of creation to the end times, when the world will be made new. It develops this by showing how the Israelites were chosen to be God's people and how the coming Messiah saves this world from sin.

The New Testament contains 27 books. They record the life of Jesus Christ the Messiah, focusing on His death, resurrection, and how He provides salvation from sin. The New Testament also records Jesus' ascension to heaven and His future return.

Different Times, Different Writers

The Bible records about 1,600 years of history. Some books were written by people who lived through and witnessed the events, while others were written by people who were not alive during those times. Some books were written in tents and prisons. Others were written in palaces. They were written by kings, prophets, poets, farmers, and apostles. Amazingly, though written by different authors, the 66 books read seamlessly because they were written by one Author.

Different Writing Styles, Methods, and Goals

The books of the Bible were written separately, but we can categorize them into groups that have similar goals and writing styles.

Types of Books in the Old Testament

Law	Genesis, Exodus, Leviticus, Numbers, Deuteronomy
	These are also known as the Pentateuch or the five books of Moses, because Moses was the author. They record the origin of all things in the world and God's promise to save humanity through Israel. It also outlines God's law to live in a relationship with Him.
History	Joshua, Judges, Ruth, 1 & 2 Samuel, 1 & 2 Kings, 1 & 2 Chronicles, Ezra, Nehemiah, Esther
	These books record the history of the kingdom of Israel, its origin, expansion, downfall, destruction, exile, and return.
Poems	Job, Psalms, Proverbs, Ecclesiastes, Song of Solomon
	These are individual experiences with God, prayers, stories, and songs.
Prophecies	Major Prophets: Isaiah, Jeremiah, Lamentations, Ezekiel, Daniel Minor Prophets: Hosea, Joel, Amos, Obadiah, Jonah, Micah, Nahum, Habakkuk, Zephaniah, Haggai, Zechariah, Malachi
	The prophets hear the voice of God and teach the people about the right way to live. Some books tell about the coming of the Christ who will save Israel. The Major Prophets and the Minor Prophets are seperated according to the size of their books.

The Old Testament Timeline

Era	Bible	Description
Creation	**Genesis 1 - 11**	This is the story of God creating the world: from Adam and Eve, the origin of sin, and the flood of Noah, to the Tower of Babel.
Patriarchs	**Genesis 12 - 50**	The patriarchs begin with Abraham and continue to Isaac, Jacob, and the story of Joseph.
Wilderness	**Exodus - Deuteronomy**	This is the story of Moses as he leads the people of Israel out of slavery in Egypt and through the wilderness. Moses receives the Ten Commandments at this time and establishes many laws.
Judges	**Joshua - 2 Samuel**	Israel conquers Canaan under Joshua's leadership, but they continue to fight against the native people of the area. Finally, David establishes a unified kingdom.
Kings	**1 Kings - 2 Chronicles**	The unified kingdom begins to worship idols during the time of Solomon. It is punished by God and split into the Southern Kingdom of Judah and the Northern Kingdom of Israel. Eventually, they are both destroyed.
Exiles	**Ezra - Nehemiah**	The people of Israel lose their kingdom and are taken as captives to Babylon. The remaining people are ruled by Babylon and Persia. Then, King Cyrus of Persia orders the rebuilding of the temple and the city walls in Jerusalem.

Types of Books in the New Testament

Gospels	Matthew, Mark, Luke, John
	These four gospels record the life and teachings of Jesus.
History	Acts
	This records the birth of the Christian church and how the gospel of Jesus Christ begins to spread throughout the world.
Epistles	Pauline Epistles (letters written by Paul): Romans, 1 & 2 Corinthians, Galatians, Ephesians, Philippians, Colossians, 1 & 2 Thessalonians, I & 2 Timothy, Titus, and Philemon General Epistles: Hebrews, James, I & 2 Peter, 1, 2, & 3 John, and Jude
	These letters, written to churches and leaders, were distributed among the Christians. Out of the 21 letters, 13 were written by Paul.
Prophecies	Revelation, parts of the Gospels and some Epistles.
	Most of the prophecies in the New Testament were written in the last book, John's book of Revelation. It tells of Jesus' second coming and how He will remove all evil and sin from creation.

The Books Are Not in Chronological Order

While the 66 books of the Bible are generally in chronological order, there are exceptions. The five books of Moses come first because they start with the creation of the world. After that, come the historical books, then the poems, followed by the prophecies.

In the New Testament the gospels appear first. They're followed by the book of Acts, which tell stories about the spreading of the gospel throughout the world. The New Testament ends with a series of letters written by Paul, other apostles, and early church leaders.

The Book of Genesis begins with the words, "In the beginning." The book of Revelation ends with the words "Come, Lord Jesus." Because all 66 books are amazingly consistent and compliment one another, it is clear they could not have been written without inspiration from God as stated in 2 Timothy 3:16. It is as if God is the conductor of a grand orchestra. Each instrument makes its own sound, but they all come together in a beautiful song.

All Scripture is inspired by God and profitable for teaching, for reproof, for correction, for training in righteousness.
- 2 Timothy 3:16

The Old Testament at a Glance

Genesis
Written: 1446-1406 B.C.
Author: Moses
God creates the world and chooses the Israelites as His special people.

Exodus
Written: 1446-1406 B.C.
Author: Moses
The Israelites, who were slaves in Egypt, are saved and led out by Moses.

Leviticus
Written: Around 1446 B.C.
Author: Moses
This describes how a sinful person can relate to God.

Numbers
Written: 1446-1406 B.C.
Author: Moses
This describes the consequences of a race that doesn't fully trust in God.

1 Chronicles
Written: Around 450 B.C.
Author: Ezra
Records the history of David's reign, focusing on worship.

2 Chronicles
Written: Around 450 B.C.
Author: Ezra
Records the history of the kings of Judah and gives hope to the people.

Ezra
Written: 457–444 B.C.
Author: Ezra
Upon returning from captivity, the people rebuild the temple and find new life in God's Words.

Nehemiah
Written: Around 420 B.C.
Author: Ezra
The people rebuild the city walls of Jerusalem and seek a righteous life.

Esther
Written: 464- 331 B.C.
Author: Unknown
The Jewish girl Esther becomes the queen of Persia and saves her fellow people.

Job
Written: Unknown
Author: Unknown
This describes the questions and answers about why good people suffer.

Psalms
Written: 1410-430 B.C.
Author: David (and others)
A songbook of praises and confessions to God.

Proverbs
Written: 950-700 B.C.
Author: Solomon
The wisdom of following God is contrasted with the destruction of following self.

Joel
Written: 835-796 B.C
Author: Joel
Judah will be restored, but only after God's judgment and their repentance.

Amos
Written: 760-745 B.C.
Author: Amos
Wrongful worship is warned against, and Amos calls for religion to be expressed in action.

Obadiah
Written: Around 841 B.C.
Author: Obadiah
The nation of Edom's destruction is prophesied.

Jonah
Written: Around 760 B.C.
Author: Jonah
God's love toward the world is revealed through the disobedient Jonah.

Micah
Written: 735–710 B.C.
Author: Micah
Micah prophesies judgment upon the leaders of Israel, but hope in the coming birth of the Messiah.

Nahum
Written: Around 640 B.C.
Author: Nahum
This describes the prophecies about the judgment upon Assyria and Nineveh.

Habakkuk
Written: Around 609 B.C.
Author: Habakkuk
God gives hope to Habakkuk's struggle over the injustice he sees in the world.

Zephaniah
Written: 635–625 B.C.
Author: Zephaniah
The Day of the Lord is prophesied, but salvation will come through repentance.

Deuteronomy
Written: Around 1406 B.C.
Author: Moses
The Law is given to a new generation that will enter the land of Canaan.

Joshua
Written: 1405-1385 B.C.
Author: Joshua
Joshua leads the Israelites into the promised land of Canan.

Judges
Written: 1050-1000 B.C.
Author: Unknown
Israel turns away from God and lives however they please.

Ruth
Written: 1011-971 B.C
Author: Unknown
Ruth, a Moabite woman, models faithfulness during the period of the judges.

1 Samuel
Written: 931-722 B.C.
Author: Unknown
This describes how the kingdom of Israel began through Samuel, Saul, and David.

2 Samuel
Written: 931-722 B.C.
Author: Unknown
The nation of Israel prospers under David's reign, but he also makes many mistakes.

1 Kings
Written: 561-538 B.C.
Author: Unknown
Solomon builds the temple but after his death, Israel is divided into the North and South.

2 Kings
Written: 561-538 B.C
Author: Unknown
Israel continues to worship idols and is eventually destroyed.

Ecclesiastes
Written: 935 B.C.
Author: Solomon
Having everything in the world is meaningless if you don't have God.

Song of Solomon
Written: 970-960 B.C.
Author: Solomon
A love song depicting the affection between a husband and wife.

Isaiah
Written: 740-680 B.C.
Author: Isaiah
Judgment for Israel is coming, but God will redeem Israel through the Messiah.

Jeremiah
Written: 627-561 B.C.
Author: Jeremiah
Jeremiah appeals for the people to repent and prophesies the coming restoration under the Messiah.

Lamentations
Written: 586-585 B.C.
Author: Jeremiah
This expresses sadness about the destroyed kingdom.

Ezekiel
Written: 593-570 B.C.
Author: Ezekiel
This describes God's judgment and salvation for the captives of Israel in Babylon.

Daniel
Written: 537-530 B.C.
Author: Daniel
Daniel, an official of Babylon and later of Persia, serves only God and prophesies the future.

Hosea
Written: 750-710 B.C.
Author: Hosea
Israel consistently betrays God, but God's love for them remains.

Haggai
Written: 520 B.C.
Author: Haggai
Haggai encourages the Jews who returned from exile to continue to follow God's Law.

Zechariah
Written: 520–518 B.C.
Author: Zechariah
Rebuilding the temple shows hope that the Messiah will come and set up His kingdom.

Malachi
Written: 433–424 B.C.
Author: Malachi
This teaches that one should repent and give true worship in preparation for the coming Messiah.

The New Testament at a Glance

Matthew
Recorded: A.D. 63-70
Author: Matthew
Jesus Christ is the Messiah and true King of Israel, as foretold in the Scriptures.

Mark
Recorded: A.D. 55-65
Author: Mark
Jesus is the Servant-Messiah and Son of God who saves the world by dying on the cross.

Luke
Recorded: A.D. 61-63
Author: Luke
Jesus helps the sick, poor, and oppressed, and He makes salvation available to every person in the world.

John
Recorded: A.D. 90-95
Author: Apostle John
Jesus shows that He is the Son of God and all who trust in Him will have eternal life.

1 Thessalonians
Recorded: A.D. 51-52
Author: Paul
Jesus' future return gives hope to pursue holiness now.

2 Thessalonians
Recorded: A.D. 51-52
Author: Paul
Paul teaches that Christ's second coming motivates action, not idleness.

1 Timothy
Recorded: A.D. 63-65
Author: Paul
Paul teaches the correct behavior for church leaders and how they should care for the church.

2 Timothy
Recorded: A.D. 63 - 65
Author: Paul
This offers encouragement to be faithful in ministry despite growing persecution.

Titus
Recorded: A.D. 63-65
Author: Paul
Churches should appoint godly leaders and teach gospel motivated conduct.

Philemon
Recorded: A.D. 61-63
Author: Paul
This is a request for an escaped slave to be forgiven and shown God's love.

Hebrews
Recorded: A.D. 64-68
Author: Unknown
This teaches that Jesus is above all creation and how He fulfills the Messianic prophecies of the Old Testament.

James
Recorded: A.D. 50-60
Author: James (brother of Jesus)
This teaches that true faith is followed by action (works).

Acts
Recorded: Around A.D. 65
Author: Luke
The Holy Spirit comes and the church begins, spreading the gospel throughout the world.

→

Romans
Recorded: Around A.D. 57
Author: Paul
Salvation is by grace through faith in the righteousness of Jesus.

→

1 Corinthians
Recorded: Around A D. 55
Author: Paul
Paul shows how the gospel fixes divisions and unrighteousness in the church.

→

2 Corinthians
Recorded: A.D. 55-56
Author: Paul
Paul defends his gospel ministry and warns against the false teachers.

↓

Galatians
Recorded: A.D. 49 or 56
Author: Paul
The gospel offers full freedom as sons and daughters of God in Christ.

←

Ephesians
Recorded: A.D. 61 - 63
Author: Paul
The gospel is by grace alone and the church is Christ's holy body.

←

Philippians
Recorded: A.D. 61-63
Author: Paul
The gospel unites all followers of Jesus in joyful unity.

←

Colossians
Recorded: A.D. 61-63
Author: Paul
Jesus is supreme over all things and supplies every spiritual need.

←

1 Peter
Recorded: A.D. 63-64
Author: Peter
Gives hope to endure in the midst of suffering by pointing to their future home of heaven.

→

2 Peter
Recorded: A.D. 63-64
Author: Peter
This teaches how to acquire true knowledge through faith, and to live a life that resembles the life of Jesus.

→

1 John
Recorded: A.D. 90-96
Author: Apostle John
Encourages Christians to love one another as God loves them.

→

2 John
Recorded: A.D. 90-96
Author: Apostle John
This teaches love and hospitality but discourages contact with false teachers.

↓

3 John
Recorded: A.D. 90 - 96
Author: Apostle John
John encourages Christian hospitality and condemns false teachers.

←

Jude
Recorded: Around A.D. 64
Author: Jude (brother of Jesus)
This teaches how to seek the truth and keep God's love within you.

←

Revelation
Recorded: A.D. 95 - 96
Author: Apostle John
John encourages believers to be faithful and turn away from sin in light of God's future judgments and final glory.

Timeline of the Kings and Prophets of Judah and Israel

The Unified Kingdom

King Saul reigned 1050-1010 B.C.
King David reigned 1010-970 B.C.
King Solomon reigned 970-930 B.C.

The Divided Kingdom

Kings and *Prophets**				Kings and *Prophets**
Judah	**Scripture**	**Dates**	**Scripture**	**Israel**
Rehoboam	1 Kings 14:21-31	**930**	1 Kings 12:25-14:20	Jeroboam
Abijam	1 Kings 15:1-8			
Asa	1 Kings 15:9-24		1 Kings 15:25-31	Nadab
		900	1 Kings 15:32-16:7	Baasha
			1 Kings 16:8-14	Elah
			1 Kings 16:15-20	Zimri
			1 Kings 16:21-28	Omri
Jehoshaphat	1 Kings 22:41-50	**875**	1 Kings 16:29-22:40	Ahab (*Elijah*)
			1 Kings 22:51-53	Ahaziah (*Elijah*)
Jehoram	2 Kings 8:16-24	**850**	2 Kings 3:1-8:15	Jehoram (*Elisha*)
Ahaziah (*Elisha*)	2 Kings 8:25-9:29		2 Kings 9:30-10:36	Jehu (*Elisha*)
Queen Athaliah	2 Kings 11:1-16			
Joash (*Joel*)	2 Kings 11:17-12:21			
			2 Kings 13:1-9	Jehoahaz (*Elisha*)
Amaziah	2 Kings 14:1-22	**800**	2 Kings 13:10-25	Jehoash (*Elisha*)
Uzziah (*Isaiah, Amos*)	2 Kings 15:1-7		2 Kings 14:23-29	Jeroboam II (*Jonah, Amos, Hosea*)
		775		
			2 Kings 15:8-12	Zechariah (*Hosea*)
Jotham (*Isaiah, Micah*)	2 Kings 15:32-38	**750**	2 Kings 15:13-15	Shallum (*Hosea*)
			2 Kings 15:16-22	Menahem (*Hosea*)
Ahaz (*Isaiah, Micah*)	2 Kings 16:1-20		2 Kings 15:23-26	Pekahiah (*Hosea*)
			2 Kings 15:27-31	Pekah (*Hosea*)
			2 Kings 17:1-41	Hoshea (*Hosea*)
Hezekiah (*Isaiah, Micah*)	2 Kings 18:1-21	**715**		
Manasseh	2 Kings 21:1-18	**700**		
		650		
Amon	2 Kings 21:19-26			
Josiah (*Jeremiah, Nahum, Habakkuk, Zephaniah*)	2 Kings 22:1-23:30			
		625		
Jehoahaz (*Jeremiah, Habakkuk*)	2 Kings 23:31-34			
Jehoiakim (*Jeremiah, Habakkuk, Daniel*)	2 Kings 23:35-24:7			
Jehoiachin (*Jeremiah, Daniel*)	2 Kings 24:8-16	**600**		
Zedekiah (*Jeremiah, Daniel, Ezekiel*)	2 Kings 24:17-25:21			

The Northern Kingdom of Israel was destroyed by King Sharmaneser V of Assyria in 722 B.C.
The Southern Kingdom of Judah was destroyed by King Nebuchadnezzar of Babylon in 586 B.C.

* (*italics*) beside a king's name shows the prophets who ministered during that time.

Find These Characters in POWER BIBLE Volumes 5 and 6

Rehoboam

Jeroboam

Elijah

Elisha

Isaiah

Jeremiah

Josiah

Hezekiah

Ahab

Daniel

2. How Old Is the Bible?

How Was It Written?

When the Bible was first being recorded, there wasn't an extensive written language as we have now. There was no paper, and printing wasn't developed. So at first, the Bible was written on stone and clay tablets. Later, it was written on animal skins and papyrus paper.

So Our Bible Is a Copy?

Although the handwritten originals are long gone, the ancient people created manuscripts by carefully copying down the text, word by word. This process is called transcribing, and it's how we got our Bible today.
The largest collection of manuscripts, the Dead Sea Scrolls were found in Israel in 1947 near the Dead Sea, in the caves of Qumran.

Khirbet Qumran

Dead Sea Scrolls

Can We Trust a Transcribed Text?

The Bible texts were copied by scribes who sincerely believed in God, so it would be unthinkable for them to change anything or put in lies. The scribes wholeheartedly committed themselves to their work. If there were any spelling errors, words added, or left out, the scribe stopped his work and started over. Because this is a holy book, the scribes were devoted to keeping it free of any errors to pass along to future generations.

What Is the Translated Bible?

The Old Testament was originally written in Hebrew. After Israel was conquered by Babylon, they were scattered throughout the world. The exiled Jews began to speak the language of their new country. As Alexander the Great expanded his empire, Greek became the common language spoken by the known world.

The first translated Bible was the Greek Septuagint. It was translated in the third century B.C. in Alexandria, Egypt, where 70 (or 72) scholars translated the Pentateuch.

During Jesus' time, this Bible was widely used. The words that Jesus spoke from the Old Testament were often from this version of the Bible.

During the age of the Roman Empire, the Bible was translated into Latin and used throughout the Middle Ages.

Latin Bible was written in 1407 in Belgium.

Even as the gospel spread throughout the world, many people still couldn't read or own a Bible. Then in 1440, Johannes Gutenberg invented the printing press eventually making the Bible more accessible to everyone.

Hebrew Original → Hebrew Transcription → Greek Translation → Latin Translation → Translated into Major Languages

The Canon and the Apocrypha

By the time Jesus was born, the 39 books of the Old Testament were completed and accepted by the Jewish community. There were additional books, known as the Apocrypha, written after the Old Testament was completed. These were not considered to be a part of the Bible.

The 27 books of the New Testament were collectively recognized as the inspired Word of God when the Council of Carthage III closed the case in A.D. 387.

The 39 books of the Old Testament, combined with the 27 books of the New Testament, make up the Bible used by the Protestant church down through the centuries.

The Bible's Journey to Us

Omni-Present God

God said to Moses, "I AM WHO I AM"; and He said, "Thus you shall say to the sons of Israel, 'I AM has sent me to you.'" - Exodus 3:14

↓

The Original Bible

God’s Word was written by human authors under the direct inspiration and control of the Holy Spirit.

↓

Bible Transcribing

There were countless hand-written copies made from the originals and then more copies made from those copies.

↓

Canonization of the Bible

Certain books that had been acknowledged for many years as the Word of God were chosen for the Bible through the process of "canonization."

39 books of the Old Testament are in the Jewish Bible.

66 books are in the Protestant Bible.

73 books are in the Catholic Bible. The seven additional books are from the non-inspired Apocryphal writings.

↓

Bible Translation

The Old Testament was originally written in Hebrew and the New Testament in Greek. Since then, the Bible has been translated into most of the languages across the world. However, there are still many people who don't have a Bible in their own language. We need to help those people by supporting Bible translation around the world.

Power Bible # 10, pg. 11

So faith comes from hearing, and hearing by the word of Christ.
- Romans 10:17

Let the word of Christ richly dwell within you, with all wisdom teaching and admonishing one another with psalms and hymns and spiritual songs, singing with thankfulness in your hearts to God.
- Colossians 3:16

For this reason we also constantly thank God that when you received the word of God which you heard from us, you accepted it not as the word of men, but for what it really is, the word of God, which also performs its work in you who believe.
- 1 Thessalonians 2:13

3. How Should I Read the Bible?

Why Should We Read the Bible?

The Bible tells us the best news in the world, that we are loved by God. Reading the stories and prophecies of the Bible shows us proof of His love. Most importantly, the Bible teaches us how we can be forgiven of our sins and made right before God. That's why the Bible is so important for us to read, over and over again.

The Bible is not a book of fairy tales or myths. It recorded historical events that help us understand our world today. It also reveals real events that will happen in the future.

Then How Should We Read It?

(1) Know the Overall Flow of the Story

The first step to understanding the Bible is to know the basic storyline. This way, we can recall a particular scene and understand where it fits into God's story of redemption. The Bible is a big book and it can be easy to get lost. But if we have a sense for the story, we won't lose sight of its main point.

(2) Read the History

History should be read in chronological order. So in order to learn the overall flow of the story of the Bible, we should read the following books in this order.

- ☐ Genesis
- ☐ Exodus
- ☐ Numbers
- ☐ Joshua
- ☐ Judges
- ☐ 1 Samuel
- ☐ 2 Samuel
- ☐ 1 Kings
- ☐ 2 Kings
- ☐ Ezra
- ☐ Nehemiah
- ☐ Luke
- ☐ Acts

(3) Connect the Branches With the Tree

History can be compared to a tree having a single trunk, with many branches and leaves. These branches and leaves are the prophecies, poems, songs, and letters that were written during the different time periods. It is easy to connect the books with the following diagram. Together, the trunk and the branches make up God's story of redemption.

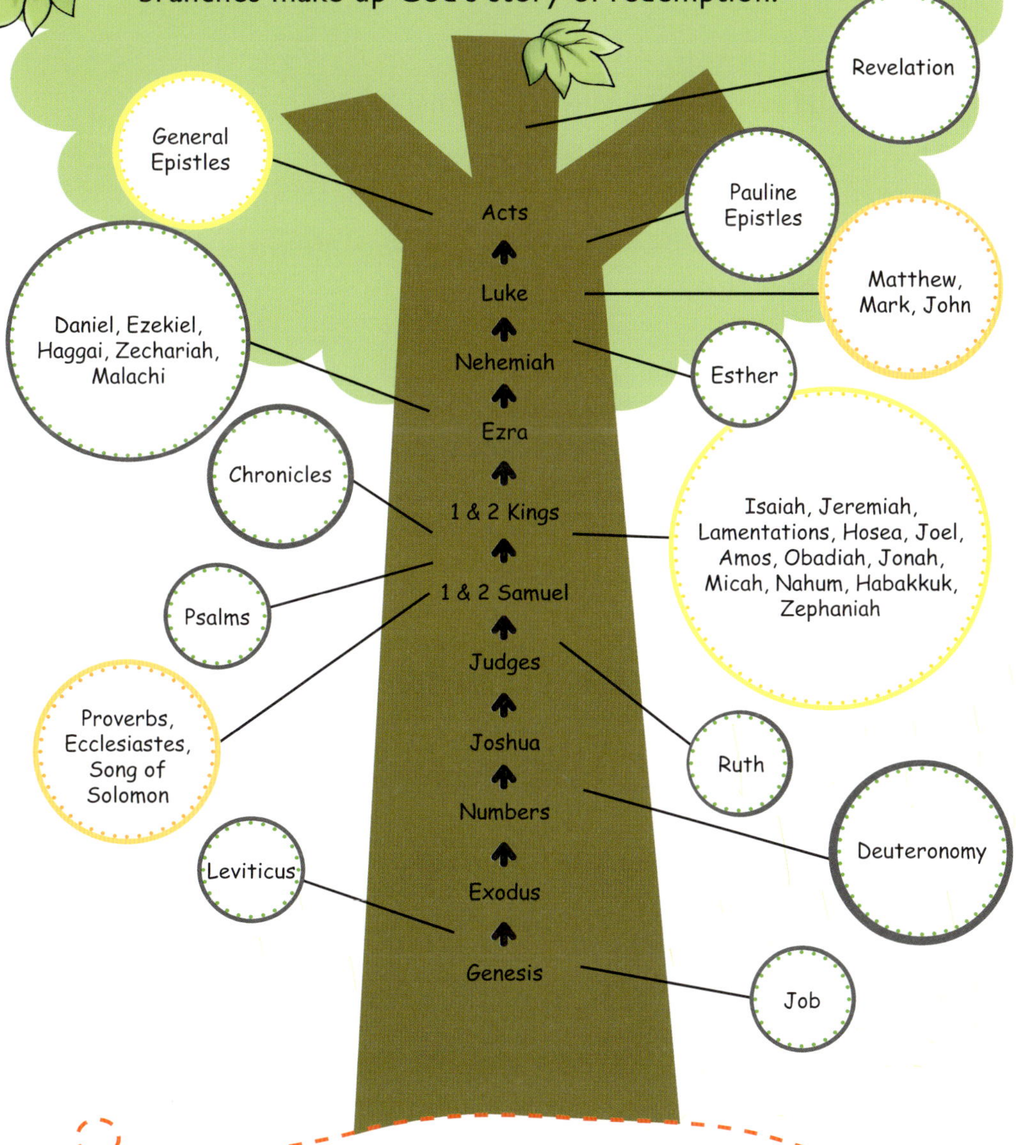

(4) Read It from Beginning to End

To really understand the Bible, we need to read it over and over again. After reading the history and connecting the prophecies, Psalms, and letters, next read it in order from beginning to end. The more you read the Bible, the easier it will be to understand. Each time you will pick up on things you previously missed, making it still interesting to read.

So How Should We Read the Bible?

First, read the thirteen historical books.

Read it quickly so that you don't lose the overall flow. Use a reading checklist of these books to stay on track.*

Second, read the rest of the books.

You can read them one at a time and in any order. But remember the time period and the history of when that book was written as you read.

Third, read it again in order from beginning to end.

*A complete checklist of every chapter in the Bible is available for free at 316publishing.com

Chapter 2

Connecting the Old and New Testaments

The Old Testament reads differently from the New Testament because they were written at different times. There are about 400 years between the end of the Old Testament and the beginning of the New Testament, even though it is just the turn-of-a-page for us. It's called the Inter-Testament Period or the Silent Years, as there were no Old Testament prophets after the death of Malachi. Before we read the New Testament, it is helpful to know what happened during this time. What did Israel experience during those 400 years?

1. The Foreign Nations That Conquered Israel

Israel's Destruction

Because of the Israelites disobedience to God's law, Babylon destroyed the city of Jerusalem and the people of Israel were taken into captivity. When the exiles returned, they rebuilt the temple and the city walls. But Israel continued to be ruled by foreign nations, including Babylon, Persia, the Greeks, and eventually the Romans.

Babylon Babylon defeated Assyria, which had destroyed the Northern Kingdom of Israel. It reached its height during the time of King Nebuchadnezzar. It attacked Jerusalem three times, taking prisoners in every assault. Finally, in 586 B.C., it destroyed Israel completely.

King Nebuchadnezzar

Persia The unified Persian Empire conquered the kingdom of Babylon during the reign of King Belshazzar. In 539 B.C., King Cyrus of Persia wrote a new law that allowed the conquered people to worship their own gods. This allowed the Israelites to rebuild the temple (during the time of Ezra) and Jerusalem's city walls (during the time of Nehemiah). The Persian Empire reached its golden years during the reign of King Darius, but it was eventually defeated by the Greeks in 330 B.C.

King Darius

Greek Empire Alexander the Great was the king who unified the Greeks and defeated the Persian Empire. In a short period of time he created one of the largest empires in world history. His empire spread Greek culture throughout the world, including Israel. While he intended to conquer the world, he died a sudden death in Babylon in 323 B.C., at the age of 32.

Antiochus IV

When Alexander the Great died, his four generals divided up the empire. They constantly fought over who would control the land of Israel, and it had many different rulers. Eventually, Antiochus IV Epiphanes ruled all of Israel. He mistreated the people, forced them to worship Greek gods, and wouldn't allow the Israelites to worship at their temple.

Hero - Judah the Maccabee (Judah Maccabeus)

When Antiochus IV forced the people to sacrifice pigs in the temple, the Priest Mattathias was enraged and led a revolt with his five sons. After the death of Mattathias, his third son Judah continued the revolt. On December 25th, 164 B.C., he finally succeeded in driving the armies of Antiochus out of Jerusalem.

Judah repaired the temple, had it purified, and made sacrifices to God according to Jewish Law. The Jewish feast of Hanukkah commemorates this day. (John 10:22)

Judah Maccabee was the first person to rise against a ruling foreign nation and win Jerusalem back since the Babylonian conquest. This led some of the Israelites to think that Judah Maccabee was the Messiah sent by God.

Rome In the third century B.C., Rome steadily gained power and began to conquer the lands of the old Greek Empire. In 65 B.C., there were three powerful generals in Rome: Julius Caesar, Crassus, and Pompey. They formed an alliance in 60 B.C. and dominated Roman politics for years. In 63 B.C., Pompey conquered Jerusalem and brought the land of Israel under Roman rule. It stayed this way until the time of Jesus.

New Powers Who Enter Judean Politics

After Israel was conquered by Rome, the people were controlled by many different Roman rulers. There were constant changes among those who held power. Let's learn about some of those figures who appear in the New Testament.

The Herodians King Herod killed all of the baby boys in Bethlehem around the time of Jesus' birth because he was afraid of the new King. But there are many other Herods who appear in the New Testament. This might be confusing at times, but they are all important figures who influenced the times of the New Testament.

- **King Herod or Herod the Great (37 B.C. - 4 B.C.)***
  He is the infamous king who ordered the killing of baby boys in Bethlehem. He wasn't Roman, but was born in Edom and made king of Judea by the Romans. He expanded the temple in an attempt to win over the people, but he died before it was completed. God sent Joseph, Mary, and Jesus to Egypt to protect them from Herod.

  Matthew 2:1-16

- **Herod Archelaus (4 B.C. - A.D. 6)**
  He was the oldest son of King Herod. After his father's death, he became the ruler of Judea, Samaria, and Edom. He was cruel just like his father and was eventually banished to France. Joseph and Mary, who fled to Egypt during the time of King Herod, went to live in Nazareth as it was prophesied because they were fleeing from Herod Archelaus.

  Matthew 2:22

- **Herod Philip II (4 B.C. - A.D. 34)**
  Also known as Phillip the Tetrarch, he was the second son of King Herod and the most decent ruler among his family. After his father's death, he became one of four rulers in Israel. He rebuilt the city of Caesarea Philippi in tribute to Caesar and himself. This is the place where Jesus asked His disciples, "Who do you say I am?"

  Mark 8:27-30

*Dates listed reflect the years they ruled.

Herod Antipas (4 B.C. - A.D. 39)
He was the youngest son of King Herod. He became the ruler of Galilee after his father's death, and he is the Herod who appears most frequently in the Bible. John the Baptist rebuked him and Jesus called him a fox. His wife, Herodias, tricked him into executing John the Baptist.

Matthew 14, Mark 6, Luke 3, 13, 23

Herod Agrippa I (A.D. 37 - A.D. 44)
He was the son of Aristobulus IV, the grandson of King Herod, and the brother of Herodias. He had the apostle James executed to win favor with the Jews. When the people called him a god and he did not correct them, God struck him down with a fatal illness.

Acts 12

Herod Agrippa II (A.D. 50 - A.D. 93)
He was the son of Herod Agrippa I. When his father died he was too young to rule over Judea. Instead, he received land in Lebanon and eventually ruled over other regions later in his life. When Paul was on trial in Caesarea, Festus invited him to participate. There Paul gave a defense of the gospel, but Agrippa II was not persuaded to believe it. He said if Paul had not appealed to Caesar, he might have been released a free man.

Acts 25, Acts 26

The Roman Emperors After Rome conquered Israel, they appointed a king to rule the lands of Judea. But when Herod Archelaus was banished, they divided up Judea into smaller territories and appointed prefects to rule the people. There are three Roman emperors and three Roman prefects who appear in the New Testament.

Augustus (27 B.C. - A.D. 14)
Augustus, also known as Octavius (Caesar Augustus), was the adopted son of Julius Caesar. He became the first emperor of Rome and received the title "Augustus," meaning "the revered one." He ordered the census that caused Joseph and Mary to go to Bethlehem where Jesus was born.

Luke 2:1

❂ Tiberius (A.D. 14 - 37)

Tiberius Augustus (Tiberius Caesar) is the stepson of Augustus and the second emperor of Rome. The ministry of John the Baptist began during the 23 year reign of this emperor.

📖 Luke 3:1-3

❂ Claudius (A.D. 41 - 54)

Claudius was the fourth emperor and he expelled Jews from Rome. Among them included Priscilla and Aquila, who would become fellow workers of Paul. A great famine in Judea also occurred during this emperor's reign, and the church in Antioch gave money to help the believers in Jerusalem.

📖 Acts 11:28

Other Romans Rulers

❂ Pontius Pilate (A.D. 26 - 36)

He was a famous Roman prefect who was just as well-known as King Herod. He conducted Jesus' trial and proclaimed His innocence. But because he was afraid of the mob, Pilate washed his hands of responsibility and agreed to have Him crucified.

📖 Matthew 27:11-26

❂ Antonius Felix (A.D. 52 - 60)

He was the procurator (in charge of financial business) who for two years kept the Apostle Paul imprisoned in Caesarea until his trial. He was known for his greediness and love for power. He married Drusilla, the daughter of Herod Agrippa I.

📖 Acts 23, Acts 24

❂ Porcius Festus (A.D. 60 - 62)

He was the procurator of Judea after Antonius Felix and he performed his duties well. He held Paul's trial and granted his request to be sent to Rome after he appealed to see the emperor.

📖 Acts 24, Acts 26

Other Religious Leaders

High Priest
The High Priest was the head of the Sanhedrin and Israel's religious leader. He was in charge of the temple and performed the sacrifices. Israel was a nation that centered around the Temple, giving the High Priest much power. However, under Roman rule, the officials were not appointed by the Jews. The High Priests Annas and Caiaphas both paid Rome to obtain their positions.

Sanhedrin
It was a council of 71 Jewish elders that had been given authority by Rome to rule over Jewish society. The members were mostly priests, scribes, Pharisees, and Sadducees. They decided on all issues that arose. Jesus and the Apostle Paul were both on trial before the leaders of the Sanhedrin.

Power Bible # 8, pg. 56

Pharisees
During the time of Jesus, the Pharisees were the strongest group among the Jews. "Pharisee" means "separate". As the name implies, these people separated themselves by adding their own rules about daily living to the Old Testament Law. While they were respected by the people for their strict lifestyle, Jesus said that they did not love God. They merely kept the Law for outward appearance.

Sadducees

This group was mostly made up of priests who worked at the temple where they made a lot of money selling animal sacrifices. They also held political power through their agreement with Rome. Unlike the Pharisees, they did not believe in the resurrection and were skeptical of any supernatural events. They were greatly despised by John the Baptist and Jesus. After Jesus overturned the money changers' tables in the temple, they sought to have Him arrested and killed.

Power Bible # 8, pg. 158

The Scribes

Sometimes called lawyers, the scribes copied the Law and taught it to the people. They believed the Scriptures were to be obeyed and followed rigidly. They enjoyed sitting in the high seats of the synagogues and being held in high esteem. Because of their pride, they were often in opposition with Jesus.

The Essenes

They were among the most devout of the Jewish groups. The Essenes did not marry and shared all of their possessions in common. They also believed that purity washings were very important. Based on the description of John the Baptist, it's possible he was a member of the Essenes.

The Zealots

The Zealots were active in their religious passion and felt it was their duty to free themselves from Rome's control. Like the Maccabees, the Zealots wanted war with whoever was ruling over them. Simon, one of Jesus' disciples, was a Zealot.

Chapter 3

The Temple and the Festivals

The Bible contains many words that we don't use today. Because it was written from the perspective of people who lived thousands of years ago, we need to learn about those people in order to properly understand the Bible. We must learn about their money, lengths, measures, and their seasons. The more we understand the history and culture of the people in the Bible, the better we will understand God's Word.

1. The Temple, the Place of Worship

The temple is where God came down to dwell with His people and it plays a central role in the story of redemption. The temple can be different things during different times. In the book of Genesis, the Garden of Eden was the temple and in Revelation, it's the New Jerusalem. In Jesus, God Himself came down. Now God dwells with His people through the Holy Spirit and the church is the temple of God. But what did worshipping God look like in the Old Testament?

1. Altar (Creation - Era of Patriarchs)

We learn about the kind of sacrifice God desires from the story of Cain and Abel. They both built altars and made sacrifices, but God only accepted Abel's, because his was made by faith. Abraham also made sacrifices. God commanded Abraham to sacrifice his only son, Isaac. By faith Abraham obeyed, and God provided a ram to sacrifice instead. God has always desired worship to be from a heart of faith that trusts in Him alone.

Power Bible # 1, pg. 69

2. Tabernacle (Wandering in the Wilderness - Era of Judges)

While wandering in the wilderness, the Israelites lived in tents and worshiped in the tabernacle. The tabernacle was a portable temple made out of tents. It needed to be easily taken down because the Israelites were constantly on the move. When the people of Israel escaped from Egypt, God used Moses to teach the Israelites how they should live and how to worship through the tabernacle. God gave them specific instructions about the materials and the making of every item within the holy tabernacle. During the wilderness wandering and the era of the Judges, the people built the tabernacle and worshipped God there.

Priest The most important role in the tabernacle belonged to the High Priest. The priests were in charge of the sacrifices and gave the people's offerings to God. The High Priest went before God to seek forgiveness for the people's sins. God assigned the priesthood to Moses' brother Aaron and his family. As the representative of the people before God, the High Priest had to be clean and blameless. He dressed in ceremonial clothes and served in the tabernacle. In the New Testament, we learn that Jesus is our perfect High Priest and our representative before God.

The Clothes of the High Priest
Exodus 28:1-43

Tabernacle Once completed, the people worshipped at the tabernacle, rather than building altars of stone. It was divided into three areas: the outer courtyard, the holy place, and the holy of holies, which only the High Priest could enter once a year. A gate on the east allowed access into the tabernacle courtyard.

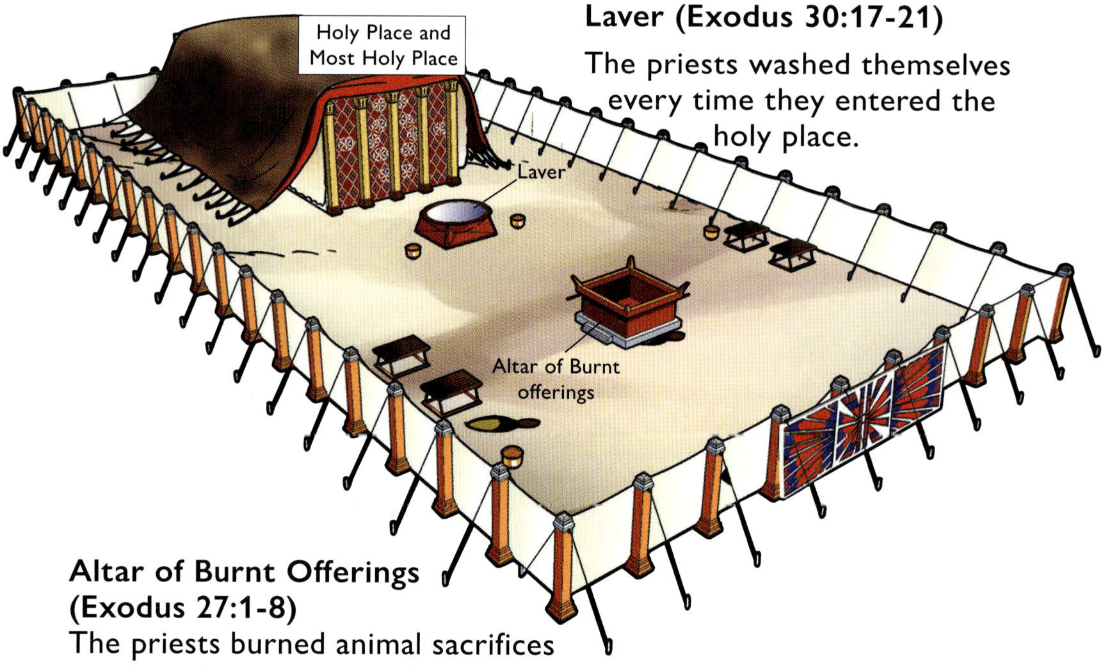

Laver (Exodus 30:17-21)

The priests washed themselves every time they entered the holy place.

Altar of Burnt Offerings (Exodus 27:1-8)

The priests burned animal sacrifices to atone for the sins of the people. The blood of the sacrificial animal was sprinkled on the altar. In the New Testament, the writer of Hebrews explains that Jesus is the perfect sacrifice whose blood was shed to forgive our sins.

Dimensions of the Tabernacle

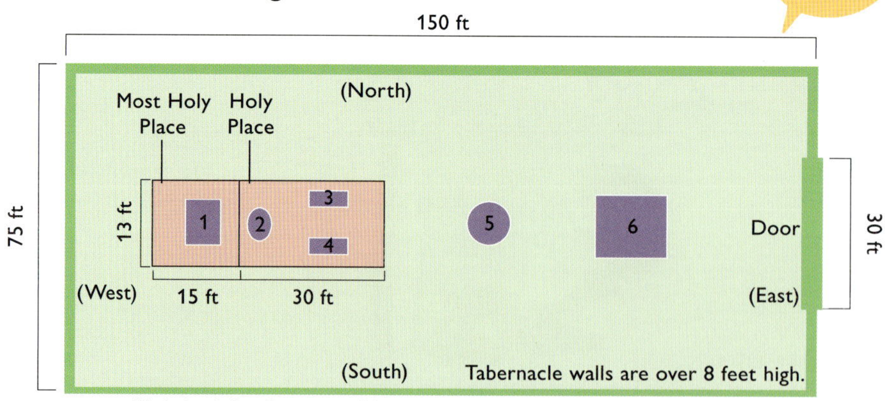

(1) Ark of the Covenant (2) Altar of Incense (3) Table of Showbread (4) Golden Lampstand (5) Laver (6) Altar of Burnt Offerings

Golden Lampstand (Exodus 25:31-40)

The lampstand had seven branches, seven lamps, and was made of pure gold. It was the priest's job to make sure the lampstand never ran out of oil.

Altar of Incense (Exodus 30:1-10)

The priests continually burned special incense here day and night.

Table of Showbread (Exodus 25:23-30)

The table was always filled with unleavened bread, which was changed on every Sabbath. It was also used for drink offerings.

Ark of the Covenant (Exodus 25:10-22)

This was in the holy of holies. Inside were the Ten Commandments, Aaron's budded rod, and a jar of manna. It was decorated with cherubim of gold on top of the ark. The space between the two cherubim was the mercy seat. It was where God came down and delivered a message to the High Priest who then declared it to the people.

What Is Ritual Sacrifice?

Because all people are born with the original sin of Adam and Eve, they cannot approach God, who is sinless. In order for the Israelites to be accepted by God, they needed to be ritually cleansed, making them free from any filth or sin. They couldn't approach God on their own merit so a sacrifice of a spotless animal had to be made on their behalf. This is how God covered the Israelite's sin in the Old Testament. The book of Leviticus describes the different types of ritual sacrifices. Today, Christians are cleansed from sin by Jesus' sacrificial death on the cross. It is through Christ that we are able to boldly approach God's throne of grace.

Types of Ritual Sacrifice in the Bible

Name	Purpose	Sacrificial Animals	Methods of Sacrifice	Description and Significance in the Bible
Burnt Offering	Atonement for sin	Male animal (bull, lamb, goat, pigeon, or turtledove) without blemish	Completely burnt on the altar	Leviticus 1:3-17; 6:8-13
Grain Offering	Offered after the burnt offering in worship and thanksgiving to God	Cooked with oil and salt along with a portion of incense	Burnt on the altar	Leviticus 2:1-16; 6:14-23
Peace Offering	A voluntary offering of thanksgiving to God	Male or female oxen, sheep, or goats—all without blemish	The animal's fat was burned and the priests ate the majority of the offering with some leftover for the worshippers	Leviticus 3:1-17; 7:11-36
Sin Offering	Given for unintentional sin or when sin is remembered	•Sins of the High-Priest: offered a bull •Sins of leaders: offered a male goat •Sins of private individuals: offers a female goat	The offering was burnt on the altar then given to the priests to eat	Leviticus 4:1-5:13; 6:24-30
Guilt Offering	Made for both sins of ignorance and omission, often atoning for robbery	Sacrifice must be equal to the value of the amount taken, plus one-fifth	The fat was burned and the remainder was eaten	Leviticus 5:14-6:7; 7:1-10

3. Temple (Unified Kingdom Era)

After settling in the land of Canaan, the 12 tribes of Israel were unified under King David and established as a kingdom. David lived in a grand palace, but the people still worshipped in the tabernacle which was made of tents. David wanted to build a beautiful and permanent house for God that wasn't old like the tabernacle.

God acknowledged David's heart, but because he was a man of war, God rejected his request. Instead, God allowed David's son Solomon to build the temple. David received the building instructions from God and gathered the materials needed for Solomon to complete the project (1 Chronicles 22, 28).

Power Bible # 5, pg. 23

Solomon's Temple

Solomon ruled over the greatest kingdom that had ever existed. He used his wealth to gather the best materials and the most skilled craftsmen. Once completed it was a beautiful temple that served as God's dwelling place (1 Kings 6).

Unlike the tabernacle, the temple was tremendous in size and made of solid rock. In the tabernacle there was one laver, golden lampstand, and table of showbread. Now there were ten of each. There was a large basin known as the Brazen Sea, and there were also two brass pillars named Boaz and Jachin, which signified God's establishment and power. When the temple was built, God told the people of Israel it would be destroyed if they did not follow His Law. This beautiful temple was destroyed in 586 B.C. by the armies of Babylon.

Zerubbabel's Temple

Power Bible # 6, pg. 21

In 539 B.C., King Cyrus of Persia conquered Babylon and sent the people of Israel back to Jerusalem. He allowed them to rebuild the temple. It was called Zerubbabel's Temple, in honor of the person who led the rebuilding project. Solomon's Temple is sometimes referred to as the First Temple, and this is referred to as the Second Temple.

The Israelites were being ruled over by Persians and there weren't enough workers for the job. So, it was less impressive than the glorious temple of Solomon. But God promised many blessings to His people through this temple (Haggai 2:3-9). However the people of Israel kept disobeying God and continued to be ruled by foreign nations. In 167 B.C., the Second Temple was greatly damaged by Antiochus IV of Syria.

Herod's Temple

Originally from Edom, Herod rebuilt the temple in order to buy the hearts of the Jews and to make them acknowledge him as their king. The outside was completed in nine years, but the entire project was not finished during Herod's lifetime. The temple was under constant construction during the time of Jesus.

This temple was much bigger than the previous temples. However, God's presence did not dwell in it. Jesus proclaimed that it would be destroyed and not one stone would be left unturned (Matthew 24:2). In A.D. 63 the temple was finally completed. But in A.D. 70, the Roman General Titus completely destroyed the temple just as Jesus had prophesied. The western wall was destroyed and today it's famously known as the Wailing Wall.

This ancient wall still stands today as one of the few remnants of Herod's Temple. It is a place where devout Jews go to pray and cry out to God.

4. Synagogue

When Babylon destroyed Israel the Jews were scattered throughout the nations. They could no longer worship in the temple to teach the Laws. New places of worship called synagogues were built and continued to be used even after the temple was rebuilt in Jerusalem. Jesus preached in the synagogues and Paul evangelized in them as well. They were different from the temple because there were no sacrifices there.

5. Church

Herod's Temple was never rebuilt after it was destroyed in A.D. 70. The original purpose of the temple was to show that God dwells with His people. It taught the people that they could have their sins forgiven and fellowship with God. But after the death and resurrection of Jesus, the sacrifices for sins were no longer necessary. Now through the Holy Spirit, God's presence dwells within everyone who trusts in Jesus (1 Corinthians 3:16). God no longer dwells in a physical building, but in the church, made up of Christians.

In whom the whole building, being fitted together, is growing into a holy temple in the Lord, in whom you also are being built together into a dwelling of God in the Spirit. - Ephesians 2:21-22

2. The Festivals and Special Days in the Bible

There are many references to festivals, special days, and seasons in the Bible that are unfamiliar to us. When we take the time to learn about them, we gain a better understanding of the Bible because they are important events in the history of Israel.

1. Israel's Seven Festivals

(1) Passover

In the first month, on the fourteenth day of the month at twilight is the Lord's Passover. - Leviticus 23:5

The Passover literally means to pass over. While the Israelites were living as slaves in Egypt, God sent plagues upon the Egyptians because He wanted Pharoah to free the Israelites. There were ten different plagues. Each time Pharaoh hardened his heart and went against God's command.

Power Bible # 2, pg. 64

Then God sent the final plague, killing the firstborn son of every person and animal in Egypt. Only the Israelites were told how to escape the plague. They were to apply the blood of a young lamb on the doorposts of their homes. The plague passed over the houses that had the lamb's blood on the doorpost and those people were spared.

Just as the blood of that lamb saved the lives of the Israelites, Jesus became the Passover Lamb by dying on the cross so that all those who believe in Him will be saved.

The next day, he saw Jesus coming to him and said, "Behold, the Lamb of God who takes away the sin of the world!" - John 1:29

(2) Feast of Unleavened Bread

Then on the fifteenth day of the same month there is the Feast of Unleavened Bread to the Lord; for seven days you shall eat unleavened bread. - Leviticus 23:6

Power Bible # 2, pg. 65

The Feast of Unleavened Bread began the day after Passover and lasted seven days. The people of Israel were not allowed to eat bread containing yeast during this time. Yeast is an important ingredient in bread that makes it rise. But when they were rushed to leave Egypt, the Israelites had to bring bread dough that had not risen. They had to eat the hard, unleavened bread until the dough ran out. God set up the Feast of Unleavened Bread to remember this day. For one week, the Jews were to eat hard, unleavened bread and bitter herbs, just as they did that fateful night in Egypt. They were to give thanks to God for rescuing their people from slavery in Egypt. To this day, the Jews eat unleavened bread, called matza, during this feast.

Unleavened Bread

(3) The Feast of First Fruits

Speak to the sons of Israel and say to them, "When you enter the land which I am going to give to you and reap its harvest, then you shall bring in the sheaf of the first fruits of your harvest to the priest." - Leviticus 23:10

During the Old Testament times, the people brought the first fruits harvested from their farms and offered them to God as an act of worship. The idea is that they take the best of their crop and sacrifice it to God. It symbolizes gratitude to God for providing the crop and trust that He will continue to provide, even though they are sacrificing their best portion. This festival is around the same time as the Passover and the Feast of Unleavened Bread, so sometimes these three festivals are all combined into the Feast of Unleavened Bread.

In the year that Jesus died, the Passover was a Friday. Jesus was resurrected in three days, so He passed away on Friday, waited through Saturday (Sabbath), and rose on the Feast of First Fruits (Sunday). Today, the church worships on Sunday to commemorate the resurrection of Jesus.

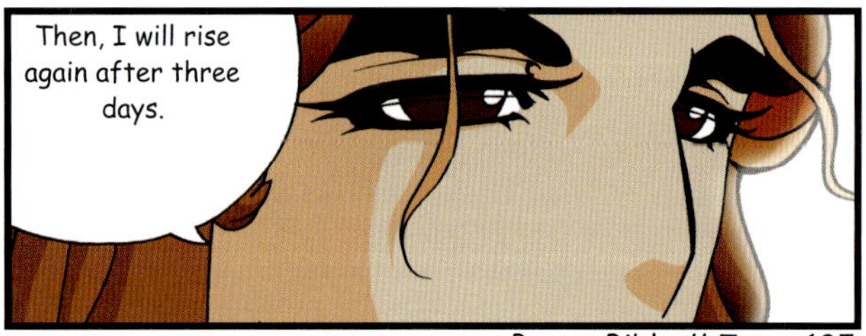

Power Bible # 7, pg. 185

But now Christ has been raised from the dead, the first fruits of those who are asleep. - I Corinthians 15:20

(4) Festival of Weeks (Pentecost)

You shall also count for yourselves from the day after the sabbath, from the day when you brought in the sheaf of the wave offering; there shall be seven complete sabbaths. You shall count fifty days to the day after the seventh sabbath; then you shall present a new grain offering to the Lord. - Leviticus 23:15-16

The Festival of Weeks has three names. It is called Pentecost, because it counts 50 days from the Feast of First Fruits. It is called the Festival of Weeks because it counts seven weeks. It is also called the Feast of Harvest because the crops are harvested. In the Old Testament, this is the day when Moses received the Ten Commandments on Mount Sinai. In the New Testament, this was the day when the Holy Spirit came upon the followers of Jesus.

When the day of Pentecost had come, they were all together in one place. And suddenly there came from heaven a noise like a violent rushing wind, and it filled the whole house where they were sitting. - Acts 2:1-2

Power Bible # 9, pg. 73

(5) Festival of Trumpets

Speak to the sons of Israel, saying, "In the seventh month on the first month you shall have a rest, a reminder by blowing of trumpets, a holy convocation." - Leviticus 23:24

The Jewish people used a lunar calendar. The first month was called Tishri. But God instructed the seventh month Nissan containing the Passover to be recognized as the first month. So the first and seventh months were both the beginning of the new year. One began the religious calendar while the other began the regular Jewish calendar.

It's just like our New Year's Day. On the first day of the seventh month, the people blew trumpets and prepared for the Day of Atonement. The people of Israel repented for their sins during the past year and tried to resolve any conflicts.

(6) Day of Atonement

On exactly the tenth day of this seventh month is the day of atonement; it shall be a holy convocation for you, and you shall humble your souls and present an offering by fire to the Lord. - Leviticus 23:27

The Day of Atonement is the most important and holy day for the people of Israel. For nine days after the Festival of Trumpets, the people repented of their sins and forgave other people. On the tenth day of the month, the people brought two goats to the High Priest. One was sacrificed to God, while the other was released into the wild.

The High Priest would take the blood of the sacrificial animal and enter the holy of holies. This was the one day out of the entire year when he was allowed to enter. On this day, the High Priest wore all white rather than his usual priestly garments. When Jesus died on the cross, the veil separating the holy of holies was torn in two, signifying that Jesus' death provides direct access to God. Jesus Himself became the sacrificial Lamb who died for the sins of the world. With Jesus' death and resurrection, animal sacrifices are no longer necessary.

By this will we have been sanctified through the offering of the body of Jesus Christ once for all. - Hebrews 10:10

(7) Feast of Booths

Speak to the sons of Israel, saying, "On the fifteenth of this seventh month is the Feast of Booths for seven days to the Lord." - Leviticus 23:34

The Feast of Booths celebrates God's protections over Israel while they wandered in the wilderness for 40 years. It is also called the Feast of Tabernacles or Sukkot. It marked the end of the harvest season. For seven days there was a celebration and on the 8th day, offerings were made to God in thanksgiving.

Many modern day Jews also build a thatched hut or tent on their property. Once the Day of Atonement is finished, they live in the tent for seven days.

Now on the first day you shall take for yourselves the foliage of beautiful trees, palm branches and boughs of leafy trees and willows of the brook, and you shall rejoice before the Lord your God for seven days. - Leviticus 23:40

On the last day of the festival, the High Priest would draw water from the pool of Siloam. As people were shouting "HOSANNA!" And trumpets were blasting, the priest would take the golden pot and pour out the water onto the altar. Jesus was present at one of these ceremonies and he cried out to the crowd, declaring Himself the "living water." He invited those who are thirsty to come to Him and drink, promising they will never thirst again.

Now on the last day, the great day of the feast, Jesus stood and cried out, saying, "If anyone is thirsty, let him come to Me and drink. He who believes in Me, as the Scripture said, 'From his innermost being will flow rivers of living water.'" - John 7:37-38

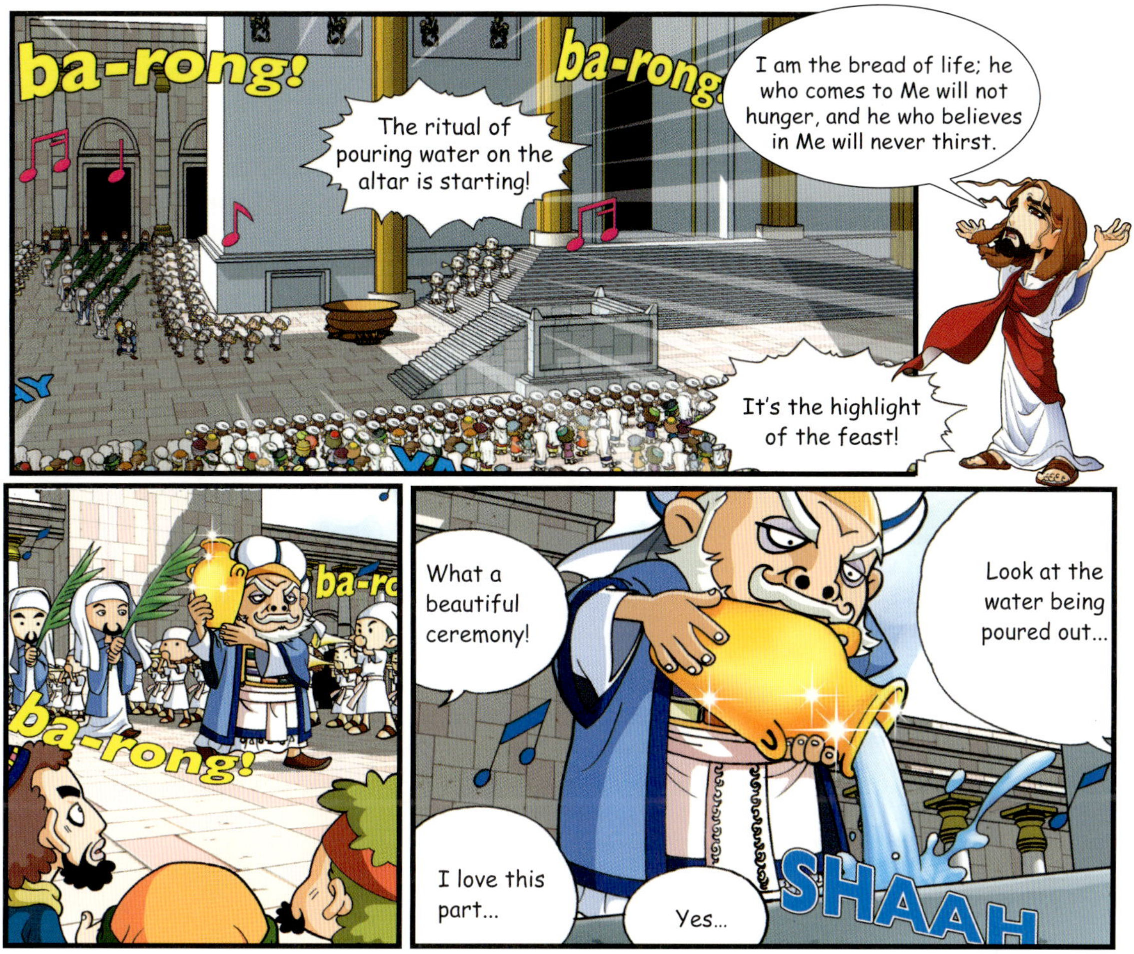

Power Bible # 8, pg. 25-27

Israel's Three Major Holidays

Just like we have several major holidays, the Israelites considered the Passover, the Festival of Weeks, and the Feast of Booths to be the most important festivals. The people of Israel were required to come to the temple in Jerusalem for these festivals to worship God. During these times, Jerusalem was filled with Jews who traveled from many other countries.

Three times in a year all your males shall appear before the Lord your God in the place which He chooses, at the Feast of Unleavened Bread and at the Feast of Weeks and at the Feast of Booths, and they shall not appear before the Lord empty-handed. - Deuteronomy 16:16

2. Festivals Created Later

God established the seven feasts of Israel. But there are two other special events in Israel's history that led to the creation of the festivals Purim and Hanukkah.

(1) Purim

Purim comes from the word "pur," which means the casting of lots. After Israel was destroyed by Babylon, thousands of Jews were taken there as captives. Among them was an orphan girl named Esther who was being raised by her cousin Mordecai. King Ahasuerus' right-hand man Haman hated Mordecai and all the Jews. He tricked the king into issuing a law that would kill them all. Haman cast lots to choose the day which all the Jews would be killed, but Esther who had become the favorite queen of the king, risked her life by revealing her identity as a Jew. Haman's plot was revealed and the king reversed his decree, executing Haman in place of Mordecai. This day became a celebration of life among the Jews and is now known as Purim.

Power Bible # 6, pg. 90

(2) Hanukkah

Hanukkah is not a biblical holiday but it's an important event in the history of Israel. When the Greeks ruled Israel, King Antiochus IV Epiphanes was a cruel ruler. In 168 B.C. he offered sacrifices to pagan gods at the Jewish temple and forced the Jews to worship the Greek gods. In response, Priest Mattathias and his five sons led a revolt against King Antiochus IV.

Judah Maccabee, one of the five sons, was especially brave and he drove the armies of King Antiochus IV out of Jerusalem. He then cleansed the temple and offered a proper sacrifice to God.

This special event is celebrated by the festival of Hanukkah. It marked the first day of Israel's independence since their exile to Babylon.

Every year at Hanukkah, the Jewish people light eight candles, one per night until all of the candles are lit on the 8th night. This represents the miracle of Hanukkah when the light in the temple did not go out for eight days, even when the lamp oil ran out.

Menorah: The candles are lit one-by-one each night until they are all lit. The large candle in the center is lit first and used to light all the other candles.

Israel's Festivals at a Glance

Israel's Seven Festivals

Name	Biblical Date	Jewish Calendar	Solar Calendar*	Meaning
Passover	1st month, 14th day	7th month	March - April	Salvation and deliverance
Feast of Unleavened Bread	1st month, 15th day for 7 days	7th month	March - April	Thanksgiving for salvation
The Feast of First Fruits	1st month, 16th day	7th month	March - April	First fruits
Festival of Weeks (Pentecost)	50th day after the Feast of First Fruits	9th month	May - June	Receiving of the Law; receiving of the Holy Spirit
Festival of Trumpets	7th month, 1st day	1st month	September -October	Reconciliation and forgiveness
Day of Atonement	7th month, 10th day	1st month	September -October	Forgiveness of sin
Feast of Booths	7th month, 15th day for 7 days	1st month	September -October	Salvation and grace

*This is the calendar we use today.

Israel's Months (Biblical Calendar)

First Month: Abib or Nisan (Exodus 13:4; Nehemiah 2:1)	Second Month: Zif (1 Kings 6:1)	Third Month: Sivan (Esther 8:9)	Fourth Month: *Tammuz*
Fifth Month: *Av* (Zechariah 8:19)	Sixth Month: Elul (Nehemiah 6:15)	Seventh Month: Ethanim (1 Kings 8:2)	Eighth Month: Bul (1 Kings 6:38)
Ninth Month: Chislev (Zechariah 7:1)	Tenth Month: Tebeth (Esther 2:16)	Eleventh Month: Shebat (Zechariah 1:7)	Twelth Month: Adar (Ezra 6:15; Esther 3:7)
Names for months in italics are not provided in the Bible.			

Festivals that Were Created Later

Name	Jewish Calendar Date	Meaning
Purim	12th month, 14th - 15th day	God saves the Jews through Esther and Mordecai
Hanukkah	9th month, 25th day	Victory against Antiochus IV Epiphanes and the reclaiming of the temple

3. Jewish Days and Times

The Jewish people also had several important days and times.

(1) Sabbath

The Sabbath was a day of rest for all people and animals. After creating the world, God rested on the seventh day. God ordered creation to follow His example and also rest one day out of the week. The seventh day in the Jewish calendar is a Saturday, so the Jews consider Saturday to be their day of rest. On this day they also remember how God saved them from slavery in Egypt.

But the seventh day is a sabbath of the Lord your God; in it you shall not do any work, you or your son or your daughter or your male servant or your female servant or your ox or your donkey or any of your cattle or your sojourner who stays with you, so that your male servant and your female servant may rest as well as you. You shall remember that you were a slave in the land of Egypt, and the Lord your God brought you out of there by a mighty hand and by an outstretched arm; therefore the Lord your God commanded you to observe the sabbath day.
- Deuteronomy 5:14-15

The Jewish religious leaders took the principle of the Sabbath and added hundreds of their own rules on how it should be followed. But when Jesus came, He didn't follow the Pharisees and Sadducees man-made rules about the Sabbath. The Jews were so caught up in "what people were allowed to do" and "what people could not do" that they forgot the original meaning of the Sabbath.

Jesus taught that adding man-made laws to the Bible was wrong. Obeying the Sabbath was something done, first and foremost, from the heart.

Power Bible # 7, pg. 92, 96-97

The Sabbath and the Week

Most Christians consider Sunday to be the day of rest rather than Saturday. The death and resurrection of Jesus fulfilled the Old Testament rituals and traditions. After Jesus rose from the dead, all days became holy, not just Saturday. Christians celebrate the resurrection of Jesus and give thanks for His grace on Sundays by worshiping Him and fellowshipping with other believers. It looks different from the Sabbath given to the Jews in the Old Testament, but the desire to worship God as a community of believers is true for both Jews and Christians.

(2) Sabbatical Year

Just as the people were commanded to rest from work every seven days, they were also commanded to rest every seven years. This was the sabbatical year. During this year, the land was allowed to rest rather than be tilled and worked for farming. All of the fruits and grains that grew naturally during that year were to be left for the poor to eat and animals to graze. Also, the peoples' debts were commanded to be forgiven in the 7th year.

Six years you shall sow your field, and six years you shall prune your vineyard and gather in its crop, but during the seventh year the land shall have a sabbath rest, a sabbath to the Lord; you shall not sow your field nor prune your vineyard. Your harvest's aftergrowth you shall not reap, and your grapes of untrimmed vines you shall not gather; the land shall have a sabbatical year.
- Leviticus 25:3-5

(3) Year of Jubilee

After seven sabbatical years, the following year was the Year of Jubilee. The Jubilee occurred every 50 years. In addition to letting the land rest, all slaves were granted freedom and allowed to return to their land. Also, all houses and lands that had been lost due to debt were returned to their original owners.

You shall have the fiftieth year as a jubilee; you shall not sow, nor reap its aftergrowth, nor gather in from its untrimmed vines.
- Leviticus 25:11

Time in the Bible

Our day starts at midnight (12 A.M.), but the Israelites started their day in the evening at sundown. This was because of the phrase in Genesis "there was evening and there was morning." In Mark, it says, "When the sixth hour came, darkness fell over the whole land until the ninth hour" (Mark 15:33). The sixth hour was actually noon, which was the brightest time of the day. That is why this is recorded as such an unusual event. Very long ago, there were no measurements for time, and it was called just day or night. So the times in the Old Testament and the New Testament are worded differently.

God called the light day, and the darkness He called night. And there was evening and there was morning, one day. - Genesis l:5

Time in the Old Testament

Name		Current Time	Example Verses
Night	First Period	Sundown - 10 P.M.	Lamentations 2:19
	Second Period	10 P.M. - 2 A.M.	Judges 7:19
	Third Period	2 A.M. - Sunrise	Exodus 14:24, I Samuel 11:11
Day	Morning	Sunrise - 10 A.M.	Genesis 24:54
	Midday	10 A.M. - 3 P.M.	Genesis 18:1, I Kings 18:27
	Afternoon	3 P.M. - 6 P.M.	Genesis 3:8
	Evening	6 P.M.	Proverbs 7:9, I Samuel 30:17

Daytime in the New Testament

Name	Synoptic Gospels* (Jewish)	Gospel of John (Roman)	Modern Time	Example Verses
Morning	0 hour	6th hour	6 A.M.	John 19:14
	3rd hour	9th hour	9 A.M.	Matthew 20:3
	4th hour	10th hour	10 A.M.	John 1:39
Midday	6th hour	12th hour	12 P.M.	Matthew 20:5
	9th hour	3rd hour	3 P.M.	Matthew 20:5
Evening	11th hour	5th hour	5 P.M.	Matthew 20:6
	12th hour	6th hour	6 P.M.	John 4:6
	1st hour	7th hour	7 P.M.	John 4:52

*The synoptic gospels are Matthew, Mark and Luke.

Nightime in the New Testament

Name	Modern Time	Example Verses
Evening	Sundown - 10 P.M.	Matthew 26:20, Mark 6:47, Mark 13:35
Midnight	10 P.M. - 1 A.M	Mark 13:35, Acts 16:25
Rooster's Crow	1 A.M. - 4 A.M.	Mark 13:35
Early Morning	4 A.M. - Sunrise	Matthew 27:1, Mark 13:35, Luke 24:1, Acts 5:21

Chapter 4

Life and Times of the Bible

The Bible was written by many writers over a very long period of time. It contains a lot of history and descriptions of the people of Israel. At times, it may be difficult for us to understand because the people in the Bible lived differently from us today. We can better understand the Bible if we understand the daily lives and culture of the people in the Bible. Let's find out about the people of the Bible together!

1. The Daily Lives of People in the Bible

1. Their Home

The Israelites were originally shepherds. They traveled with their flock to the grazing areas. During the times of Abraham and Moses, they lived in tents that were easy to transport. Later, they settled in Canaan and began to farm. They built houses that would protect them from the desert sun and sandstorms.

Tents

After their escape from Egypt, and during the 40 years of wandering in the wilderness the Israelites lived in tents surrounding the tabernacle. They raised wooden poles and covered them in fabric made from animal skin.

Power Bible # 2, pg. 180

Houses

The people began to build houses after they settled down and began to farm. Wealthy people built houses with multiple rooms or a second floor. For most people, their home was a small earthen house or cave with just a few rooms.

Power Bible # 9, pg. 83

Some of the cities in Israel were built in high locations to prevent enemies from attacking them. The people built their houses inside the city walls. They needed firm foundations to protect themselves from earthquakes and floods in the area. Some homes used stones for building material, while others used bricks made from dirt. The entrances were low to protect against the sun and sandstorms, and the windows were small.

Roof

The Israelites' houses had flat roofs and on hot summer nights they would even sleep there. They were sometimes used for storage (Joshua 2:6) or for people to stand on and proclaim important information (Matthew 10:27). People also went up to the roof to pray (Acts 10:9). During Old Testament times, people set up idols on the roof and suffered God's wrath (Jeremiah 32:29).

Power Bible # 9, pg. 148

Cornerstone

This was a large stone that connected two walls. The cornerstone was the most important part of a building because it kept it secure. Because of its importance, they used the strongest stones. This became an analogy for Jesus, who is the cornerstone of the church (1 Peter 2:4-8).

Jesus said to them, "Did you never read in the Scriptures, 'The stone which the builders rejected, this became the chief cornerstone; this came about from the Lord, and it is marvelous in our eyes'?" - Matthew 21:42

He is the stone which was rejected by you, the builders, but which became the chief cornerstone. - Acts 4:11

2. The People's Food

The Bible talks a lot about the food that the people ate. The Old Testament law prescribed certain foods that they could eat and certain foods they could not eat. Also, Jesus' sermons contain many references to grains and fruits. So what did the people of Israel eat?

Common Products of Canaan

A land of wheat and barley, of vines and fig trees and pomegranates, a land of olive oil and honey. - Deuteronomy 8:8

- **Wheat and Barley:** These were ground with a millstone to make bread.

- **Olives:** Olive trees are very common in Israel. The Mount of Olives, where Jesus prayed in the Garden of Gethsemane, means "oil press." The Israelites harvested oil from the olives.

- **Grapes:** When Moses sent twelve men to spy out the land of Canaan, they came back with grapes. This is one of Israel's most abundant fruits.

- **Pomegranates:** Pomegranates are another common fruit in Israel. The scouts of Canaan also came back with pomegranates.

- **Figs:** This is a sweet fruit that was often used as an analogy for the land of Israel.

- **Honey:** The land of Canaan is described as a land flowing with milk and honey. It means that the fruits of the land God gave the Israelites were as nutritious as milk and as sweet as honey.

Power Bible # 7, pg. 155

Bread of Life

Just as many cultures have staple foods they often eat, such as rice, beans, or pasta, bread was the common food among the Israelites. Because of its importance in their daily diet, bread had a special significance. It was as important as life itself. Bread was considered to be the "manna" that God provided to the Israelites for 40 years in the wilderness. Knowing the importance of bread, Jesus calls himself the "living bread" (John 6:51). Just as we need to eat physical bread to stay alive, we daily need Jesus in order to spiritually live.

Meat and Fish

The Israelites also ate meat and fish. Because they were the holy people of God, the Old Testament Law outlined some animals that were considered clean and could be eaten, and others that were unclean and could not be eaten. The Sea of Galilee provided plenty of fish for the entire nation. It was preserved by salt and sold throughout Israel.

Name	Clean (can be eaten)	Unclean (cannot be eaten)
Animal	Animals that chew the cud and have cloven hooves	Camels, hyrax, hare, pig
Fish	Must have fins and scales	Those with neither fins nor scales
Bird	No specific rules	Eagle, vulture, kite, falcon, raven, ostrich, hawk, seagull, owl, cormorant, stork, heron, hoopoe, bat
Insect	Certain kinds of winged insects	Winged insects that have four feet

Miracle of the Multiplying Fish

Jesus performed many miracles. He healed the sick, walked on water, and even raised the dead. He also fed thousands of people with just five loaves of bread and two small fish.

One day, many people had gathered near the Sea of Galilee to hear Jesus preach. Just the men numbered more than 5,000 and there were many women and children as well. But they only had five pieces of barley bread and two small fish to eat. The disciples wanted to get more food, but Jesus told them that this was enough. He gave thanks for the food and told His disciples to distribute the bread and fish. Everyone ate their fill and there were twelve baskets of leftovers. This is the miracle of multiplication (Matthew 14:14-21). It signifies that Jesus truly is the bread of life (John 6:35).

Power Bible # 7, pg. 144-145

The Israelites' Meals

Food was a central part of the Jewish culture. The Bible is full of stories that involve preparing food and eating meals. Jews would frequently show hospitality to traveling strangers by inviting them to eat as a guest. Jesus and His disciples regularly ate as guests while traveling from town to town. The gospels tell about Jesus' last meal with His disciples, where He commanded them to receive the bread and wine as a way of remembering His sacrificial death on the cross. The resurrected Jesus prepared a breakfast of fish for the disciples who had been fishing all night (John 21:12-13). The Bible also describes a feast for all the citizens of heaven to enjoy (Isaiah 25:6-9).

Power Bible # 9, pg. 63

The Israelites ate two meals, one in the morning and one in the evening. Breakfast was simple, but dinner was a big and happy meal. Teachings and debates often occurred during this time.

Power Bible # 8, pg. 186

3. Clothes in the Bible

Just like us, the clothes the Israelites wore were designed with the weather in mind. Because Israel has a desert climate, it is very hot during the day, but cold at night. The clothes they wore had to work for both temperatures. A person's status or job was also reflected in their clothes.

Status or work affected a person's clothing, but for most people during this time, there was always an outer cloak, a tunic, a belt, and sandals.

Typical Daily Clothing

Outer Cloak

The cloak was a regularly used piece of clothing. The Israelites often slept outside at night while traveling, so the cloak was used as a blanket to keep them warm. Most people could not afford multiple cloaks, so if someone lent you their cloak, you were told to return it before sundown (Exodus 22:26).

Power Bible # 5, pg. 103

Elijah gives his cloak to Elisha and makes him the next prophet (1 Kings 19:19).

Tunic (Undergarment)

This was a loose-fitting item like a long t-shirt that was always worn, regardless of the season. The wealthy could afford tunics of fine linen and purple cloth. However, the poor had tunics made from rough animal hair. It was often very big and required a belt.

Women wore their tunics down to their ankles. Men wore their tunics to their knees. The wealthy and powerful people often wore long tunics and cloaks.

Belt

Belts were made of fabric or leather and often were a symbol of a person's wealth. The rich wore belts that were over 13 feet long and carried their money in them. During times of war, weapons were also carried in belts.

Power Bible # 3, pg. 159

Sandals

The Jews often wore sandals instead of shoes. They were made of palm tree bark or leather. John the Baptist said that he was not worthy to untie the strap of Jesus' sandals (John 1:27). Sandals had a special significance. Taking off a sandal and giving it to another person transferred your property or obligation to that person. On the other hand, the one with the sandal had rights. It was also customary to have a servant take off your sandals and wash your feet if you entered someone's house as their guest.

Turban

Because of the heat, the Israelites wore turbans to protect themselves from the sun. The fabric was like a towel, wrapped around one's head and secured with string. Women also wore veils when they went outside to hide their head and face.

Staff

The staff had various uses and meanings in the Bible. It was a necessary item for a traveler and it was used by shepherds to guide and protect their sheep. Kings and leaders also had staffs to show their authority. Prophets carried staffs to show God's power and judgment.

King Ahasuerus holds out his staff toward Esther to show his authority as king (Esther 5:2).

God displayed His power and authority through the staff of Moses.

4. Jobs in the Bible

Power Bible # 7, pg. 44

As their society grew the different types of jobs also increased. Although thousands of years separate us from them, the jobs we have today aren't that different from theirs. Among Jesus' disciples, Peter, Andrew, John, and James were fishermen. Matthew was a tax collector, and the gospel-writer Luke was a doctor. Like today, jobs were often passed down through families. Before Jesus began His ministry, He was probably a carpenter like His father Joseph. The most respected jobs in Israel were the clerks and teachers of the Law. They were called Rabbi, Father, and Lord. But Jesus despised the teachers who did not teach the true meaning of the Law. Instead, He associated with people who were considered beneath others in status, such as tax collectors and shepherds. Jesus became a friend to those whom society considered to be outcasts.

Jobs Found in the Bible

Job Type	Example Verse	Job Type	Example Verse
Artisan	Proverbs 26:10	Overseer	Genesis 39:4
Carpenter	I Chronicles 22:15, Matthew 13:55	Politician	Daniel 3:2-3
Cook	I Samuel 8:13	Potter	Jeremiah 18:1-4
Coppersmith	2 Timothy 4:14	Jailer	Acts 16:23, Genesis 39:22
Doctor	Colossians 4:14	Record Keeper (Historian)	2 Samuel 8:16
Fabric Seller	Acts 16:14	Sailor	Jonah 1:5, Acts 27:27
Farmer	Genesis 9:20	Scribe	I Corinthians 1:20
Fisherman	Mark 1:16	Secretary	2 Samuel 8:17
Gardener	John 20:15	Shepherd	I Samuel 17:15, Luke 2:8
Gatekeeper	2 Samuel 18:26 Ezra 10:24	Soldier	2 Timothy 2:4
Goldsmith	Nehemiah 3:32	Steward	Genesis 43:16, Luke 8:3
Lawyer	Luke 10:25	Tanner	Acts 9:43
Merchant	Nehemiah 13:20	Tax Collector	Matthew 9:9
Messenger	2 Kings 14:8	Teacher, Rabbi	Matthew 23:7-8
Money Changer	John 2:14, Mark 11:15	Tent-maker	Acts 18:3
Moneylender	Exodus 22:25, Psalms 109:11	Treasurer	Ezra 1:8
Musician	Psalm 68:25	Vineyard Worker	Matthew 21:28

Power Bible # 8, pg. 120

5. Measurements in the Bible

Lengths and measurements weren't fully developed during the time of the Bible and they were quite a bit different than the systems used today. Though not exact, they were close to being the same down through the centuries of the Bible. This conversion chart will help explain the language used for measurements in the Bible.

Lengths

Name	Length	Example Verses
Finger	3/4 inch	Jeremiah 52:21
Handbreadth	3 inches	I Kings 7:26
Span	almost 9 inches	Exodus 28:16
Cubit	18 inches	Genesis 6:15
Fathom	6 feet	Acts 27:28
Stadion	200 yards	Matthew 14:24
One Day's Journey	Around 20 miles	Numbers 11:31
Sabbath's Day Journey	2/3rds of a mile	Acts 1:12

Types of Money

Persian Shekel of King Darius

Category	Name	Value	Verse Examples
Jewish	Gerah	1/20 of a shekel	Exodus 30:13
	Beka	1/2 of a shekel	Exodus 38:26
	Shekel	1 Gold = 15 silver 1 Silver = 4 days' average wages	1 Chronicles 21:25 Matthew 17:27
	Talent	1 Gold = 15 silver 1 Silver = 6,000 bekas	1 Chronicles 29:4, Matthew 18:24
Roman	Quadrans	1/64 of a denarius	Matthew 5:26
	Assarion	1/16 of a denarius	Matthew 10:29
	Denarius	One day's wages	Matthew 18:28
Greek	Lepta	1/128 of a denarius	Mark 12:42, Luke 12:59
	Drachma	One day's wages	Luke 15:8

Drachma of Alexander the Great

◉ Weights

Name	Weight	Verse Example
Gerah	0.02 oz. (1/20 of a shekel)	Exodus 30:13
Shekel	0.4 oz. (about ½ oz.)	2 Samuel 14:26
Mina	20 oz. (l lb. 4 oz.)	Luke 19:13-25
Talent	About 75 lbs. (3000 shekels)	Exodus 38:25

6. Lives of the Ancients from Birth to Death

Important moments in everyone's life are birth, growth, marriage, and death. For the Christian it also includes the day they received the gospel. The Israelites were called to live their lives in a way that would glorify God. So how did the people of Israel live?

(1) Birth: Children Are Blessings from God

God told Adam and Eve to "be fruitful and multiply" (Genesis 1:26) and the role of child-bearing is a God-given honor. But because of sin it's now marked by pain and suffering. In Jewish culture, childless wives like Sarah and Elizabeth were looked down upon. But God answered their prayers and they were blessed with sons. God promised that a baby would be born who would crush Satan and destroy all evil (Genesis 3:15). Jesus' birth fulfilled that promise.

Power Bible # 7, pg. 35

(2) Growth: Circumcision and Naming

Power Bible # 1, pg. 115

After a male baby was born, he was circumcised on the 8th day. It was a sign of the covenant of Abraham and marked him as a member of Israel. Babies were also given their name on the 8th day. Names were significant in the Bible because the meaning behind the names often became a personal character trait throughout their life.

Power Bible # 7, pg. 47

(3) Growth: Education

Education in Israel was very important, because children needed to study the Law. Their education started with memorizing the Law of Moses. As soon as a child started talking, he or she learned the verse "Hear, O Israel! The LORD is our God, the LORD is one!" This is what God commanded Israel to do in Deuteronomy 6:7.

> You shall teach them diligently to your sons and shall talk of them when you sit in your house and when you walk by the way and when you lie down and when you rise up. - Deuteronomy 6:7

Power Bible # 7, pg. 191

When the children were young, their education was mostly from their mother. As they grew older, their father became more involved. It was common for rabbis to teach children in the synagogues and their homes. During the time of Jesus, Jewish children learned math, writing, and the Mosaic Law. There also were special schools for higher learning to train youth to become scholars of the Law. Paul states that he was taught by the famous scholar Gamaliel. The rabbis usually taught through repetition, memorization, and by asking questions. Not all of them agreed with one another on the interpretation or application of the Scriptures.

Power Bible # 1, pg. 100

Power Bible # 8, pg. 155

Power Bible # 1, pg. 115

(4) Marriage - The Greatest Festival

In Israel, marriages were arranged between families. For example, Abraham sent his servant to find a wife for his son Isaac from his hometown. There was an engagement period called the betrothal. Unlike our engagement practices today, being betrothed equalled being married. On the wedding day, there was a feast for the couple with family and friends and the celebration could last up to a week.

(5) Death

In Bible times, different people groups had different beliefs about death. For example, the Egyptians believed in an afterlife and were not afraid of death. They believed that the body had to be prepared for passage into the next world. So after death, they mummified the body and prepared the tomb as if a living person would reside there. The Israelities had their own burial practices. They wrapped the body in linen and placed them in a tomb. The tomb was dug into a hillside or cave. It was often closed with a stone door.

Model of Jesus' Tomb in Jerusalem

7. Poor People in the Bible

The poor people in the Bible were the sick, the disabled, the orphans, and the widows. Medicine was not well developed, so sickness was more common than it is today and often untreatable. Unfortunately, many wrongly believed the sick and poor were being punished by God.

Women and children were the least acknowledged people in Bible times. They had no rights and could not testify to anything. But Jesus healed the sick and the disabled and became a friend to the widows and orphans. They could now live confidently as sons and daughters of God.

Power Bible # 8, pg. 52

Power Bible # 8, pg. 95

2. Israel's Region

(1) Israel's Geography

Israel is strategically located between the ancient civilizations of Mesopotamia and Egypt. It sits on the Mediterranean Sea, which is directly to the west. It is a land bridge between three major continents, Africa, Asia, and Europe. The location is so central that many powerful nations fought to own the land of Israel. The geography of Israel is divided into the Coastal Plains, the Central Hills, the Jordan Rift Valley, the Negev (southern plains), and the Trans-Jordan Plateau.

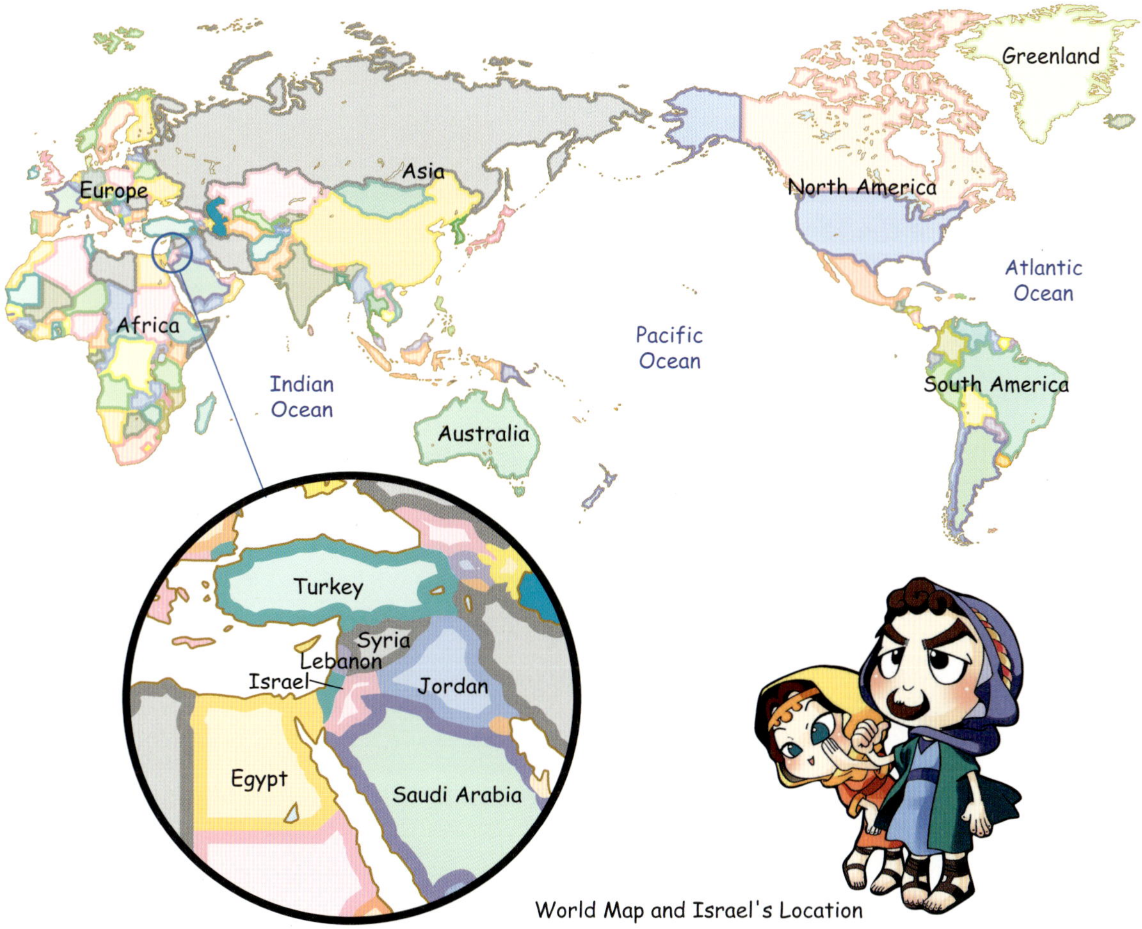

World Map and Israel's Location

Israel's Regions

- **Coastal Plains:** The Coastal Plains are on the western edge of Israel, up against the Mediterranean Sea. The flat ground provided a common highway between Egypt and Europe. The term "valley" in the Bible often refers to this area.
- **Central Hills:** The Central Hills, or the Hill Country are the high central areas of Galilee, Mount Ephraim, and the Judean Hills.
- **Jordan Rift Valley:** This is near Mount Hermon where the Jordan River begins. It includes the Sea of Galilee and the Dead Sea, all the way down to the Gulf of Eilat. This is the lowest point of elevation in the world.
- **The Negev:** This is a flat desert to the south. Beersheba is the last livable place here.
- **Trans-Jordan Plateau:** This is the area from Mount Hermon to the area east of the Jordan River and down to the Red Sea. This region is also known as the Western part of Jordan. It flows through the Amon and Jabok Rivers, down into the Dead Sea.

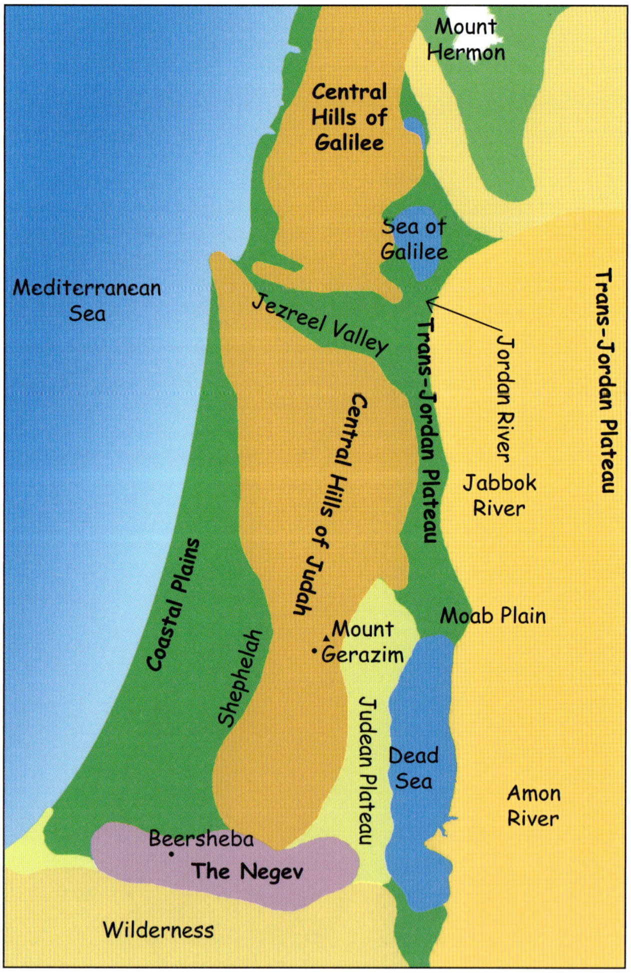

Israel's Geography

Sea of Galilee

Water was precious in Israel so the Sea of Galilee was very important. It is a large body of fresh water, similar to a lake. It was also called Gennesaret or Tiberias. The Israelites relied on fish caught from this lake. Jesus spent a lot of time in this area.

2. Israel's Climate

Israel has a Mediterranean climate with long, hot, dry summers and relatively short, cool, rainy winters. The rainwater would seep into the ground to create springs which helped the people endure the hot summers.

That He will give the rain for your land in its season, the early and late rain, that you may gather in your grain and your new wine and your oil. - Deuteronomy 11:14

What Is the Early Rain and Late Rain?

The early rain came in October and November. It softened the ground and allowed farmers to plant seeds. The late rain came at the end of winter in March and April. This helped the crops to ripen. If either the early or late rain was too strong, the crops would be ruined. The Israelites relied upon God to provide just the right amount of rain they needed in order for their crops to survive.

Power Bible # 3, pg. 86

During the summer, it didn't rain for many months and the weather turned into a desert climate. Dew formed from the temperature difference going from day to night and it was vital for them to survive. The people considered the dew to be a blessing from God.

Pagan Weather Idols

The Israelites were focused on rainfall for the crops to grow and water for themselves and their livestock. The idols of the false rain gods drew the hearts of the people away from the true God. In the Old Testament, the Canaanite gods Baal and Asherah were related to weather. As the Israelites started to farm in Canaan, they began to worship Baal and Asherah because they believed these gods affected their harvests. They suffered greatly and even lost their kingdom because they refused to let go of these idols.

Baal: This male Canaanite god was considered the god of the rainstorm. He holds a hammer in his right hand and a lightning-like spear in his left hand.

3. Israel's Vegetation in the Bible

Olive Tree (Exodus 23:11)

Fig Tree (Mark 11:13)

Grapevine (Deuteronomy 23:24)

Palm Tree (John 12:13)

Shittah (Acacia) Tree (Exodus 25:10)

Shrubs (Exodus 3:4)

Pomegranate Tree (Numbers 13:23)

Almond Tree (Genesis 30:37)

Thorn Bush (Judges 9:14)

Poplar Tree (Genesis 30:37)

Willow Tree (Genesis 30:37)

Juniper Tree (1 Kings 19:4)

Carob Tree (pods) (Luke 15:16)

Mustard Tree (Luke 13:19)

Lily of the Valley (Matthew 6:28)

Papyrus (reeds) (Exodus 2:3)

Hyssop (Exodus 12:22)

Frankincense (Matthew 2:11)

Fennel (Dill) (Isaiah 28:25)

Rue (Luke 1:42)

Myrrh (Exodus 30:23)

Iris (Song of Solomon 4:14)

Thistle (Genesis 3:18)

Mint (Luke 11:42)

Mandrake (Genesis 30:14)

Israel's Timeline at a Glance

The Bible contains many events over many long years. The timeline is not always exact, especially for events before the birth of Jesus. This is a rough timeline to keep in mind as you read the Bible.

Old Testament (B.C.)

	God creates the world and everything in it.
2500 B.C.	The Great Flood occures. Noah and his family
2166 B.C.	Abraham is born.
2091 B.C.	Abraham leads his family out from Ur of the Chaldeans and into Canaan.
2066 B.C.	Abraham has his son Isaac at the age of 100.
2006 B.C.	Isaac and Rebekah have the twins Esau and Jacob.
1991 B.C.	Abraham dies and is buried in the Cave of the Patriarchs in Hebron.
1906 B.C.	Jacob wrestles with God and his name is changed from Jacob to Israel.
1898 B.C.	Joseph, the son of Jacob and Renekah, is sold as a slave by his brothers and taken to Egypt.
1886 B.C.	Joseph becomes prime minister of Egypt.
1875 B.C.	Jacob and his family move to the land of Goshen in Egypt.
1806 B.C.	Jacob dies in Goshen and is buried in the Cave of the Patriarchs.
1806 B.C.	Joseph dies.
1525 B.C.	Moses is born to Amram and Jochebed.
1446 B.C.	Moses is called by God at the age of 80.
1446 B.C.	Moses parts the Red Sea and leads the people of Israel out of Egypt.
1446 B.C.	Moses receives the Laws of God and builds a tabernacle as God instructs.
1406 B.C.	Moses dies and Joshua takes over. He leads the Israelites into Cannan.
1375 B.C.	Joshua dies.
1375 B.C.	Judges begin to rule the people.
1100 B.C.	Hannah's prayer is answered and Samuel is born.
1050 B.C.	At the people's request, Samuel anoints Saul as the new king of Israel.
1010 B.C.	David becomes king over all of Israel.
990 B.C.	Solomon is born to David and Bathsheba.
970 B.C.	David dies and Solomon becomes king.
959 B.C.	Solomon completes construction of the First Temple in seven years.
931 B.C.	Solomon dies and Israel divides into the Northern and Southern Kingdoms.
874 B.C.	Ahab becomes King of Israel. Elijah defeats the priests of Baal.
851 B.C.	Elijah is taken to heaven in a storm of fire. His disciple Elisha receives his power.
740 B.C.	The prophet Isaiah begins his ministry during the time of King Uzziah.

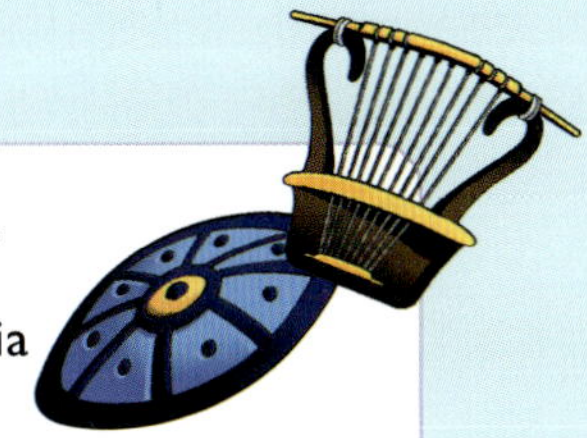

722 B.C.	The Northern Kingdom of Israel is destroyed by Assyria.
715 B.C.	King Hezekiah's reign brings repentance.
701 B.C.	During the reign of King Hezekiah, Sennacherib of Assyria besieges Jerusalem, but God causes him to withdraw.
628 B.C.	King Josiah institutes religious reform.
627 B.C.	Jeremiah is called to be a prophet.
609 B.C.	King Josiah is killed in battle against Pharaoh-Necho of Egypt.
605 B.C.	Nebuchadnezzar of Babylon attacks the people of Judah. Daniel and his friends are taken as captives.
597 B.C.	Babylon attacks for the second time. The people of Judah, including Ezekiel, are taken as captives.
586 B.C.	Babylon attacks for the third time and Jerusalem falls. More people are taken away as captives.
580 B.C.	Daniel's friends survive the fiery furnace.
562 B.C.	King Nebuchadnezzar of Babylon dies.
539 B.C.	Babylon is defeated by King Cyrus of Persia.
538 B.C.	Daniel survives the lion's den during the reign of King Darius.
537 B.C.	The captives return from Babylon and begin to rebuild the city of Jerusalem and the temple under orders from King Cyrus.
515 B.C.	The Second Temple (Zerubbabel's Temple) is completed.
478 B.C.	Esther becomes the queen of the Persians.
473 B.C.	Esther and Mordecai save the people of Israel, and the Festival of Purim begins.
458 B.C.	Ezra and the captives return to Jerusalem.
445 B.C.	The captives return for the third time, and the city walls are rebuilt under Nehemiah's leadership.
430 B.C.	The Old Testament's last prophet Malachi begins his ministry.

Inter-Testament Period

After Malachi, there were no prophets for about 400 years. This period is also called the Dark Period. Then, John the Baptist appeared as Malachi had foretold, proclaiming that the Messiah had come.

New Testament (A.D.)

5 B.C.	Jesus is born.
A.D. 8	Jesus visits Jerusalem during the Passover at the age of 12.
A.D. 14	Tiberius becomes the emperor of Rome.
A.D. 26	John the Baptist begins his work.
A.D. 27	Jesus begins His ministry.
A.D. 28	Jesus chooses His twelve disciples.
A.D. 29	Jesus feeds 5,000 men on the plain of Bethsaida.
A.D. 30	Jesus dies on the cross and resurrects from the grave.
A.D. 30	The Holy Spirit comes upon the believers in the upper room.
A.D. 33	Saul goes to Damascus to capture Christians but is converted on his journey.
A.D. 36	Paul visits Jerusalem and meets Barnabas and James.
A.D. 37	Paul embarks on his first missionary journey.
A.D. 41	The apostle James is executed by Herod Agrippa.
A.D. 48	Paul attends the religious council in Jerusalem.
A.D. 50	Paul embarks on his second missionary journey.
A.D. 53	Paul embarks on his third missionary journey.
A.D. 54	Nero becomes the Emperor of Rome.
A.D. 54	Paul is arrested in Jerusalem and transferred to Caesarea.
A.D. 62	Paul is under house arrest in Rome.
A.D. 64	There is a great fire in Rome and Nero begins to
A.D. 64	persecute the Christians.
A.D. 67	Paul is martyred.
A.D. 68	Peter is martyred.
A.D. 70	The Roman General Titus invades Jerusalem and destroys the temple.
A.D. 95	The apostle John is exiled in Patmos and writes the book of Revelation.
A.D. 100	The apostle John dies.

AN INTRODUCTION TO READING THE BIBLE

POWER BIBLE Guidebook

Published by: Green Egg Media, a division of Three Sixteen Publishing Inc.
316publishing.com

Originally published in Korea by Mirae N Co., Ltd. (I-seum)
This translated edition was published by arrangement with Mirae N Co., Ltd. (I-seum)

PB0015
ISBN 978-1-937212-64-3
Printed in Korea by Codra Enterprises, Inc. codra.com

Green Egg Media a division of THREE SIXTEEN PUBLISHING

POWER BIBLE

FREE DOWNLOADS!

Guide Samuel to David

Directions for Activity

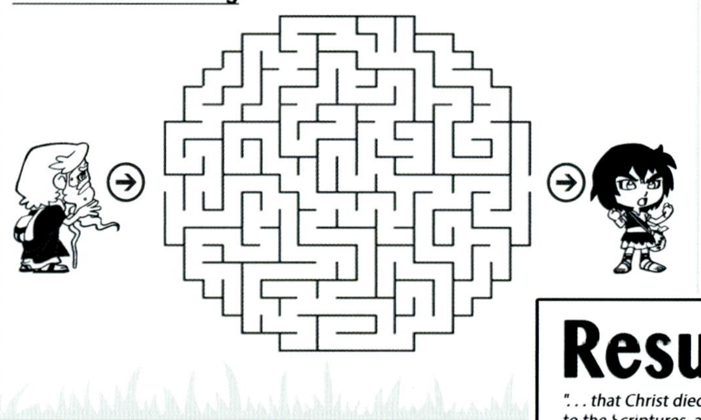

Old & New Testament
Activity & Coloring Packets!

OVER 50 PAGES!
ALL FREE!

Resurrection

". . . that Christ died for our sins according to the Scriptures, and that He was buried, and that He was raised on the third day according to the Scriptures, and that He appeared to Cephas, then to the twelve. After that He appeared to more than five hundred brethren at one time, most of whom remain until now, but some have fallen asleep; then He appeared to James, then to all the apostles." 1 Corinthians 15:3-7

Directions for Activity

Search the words listed below!

Word Bank:

Christ	Raised	
Died	Appeared	Brethren
Sins	Cephas	James
Scriptures	Twelve	Apostles
Buried	More	

S	K	I	E	T	D	E	D	E	B	W	J
K	C	F	U	V	W	I	R	R	F	W	A
E	A	R	E	F	E	E	E	O	D	D	M
C	P	A	I	D	T	T	L	E	M	E	E
E	P	U	V	P	H	S	S	V	M	I	S
A	E	T	W	R	T	I	I	W	E	R	M
Z	A	L	E	N	A	U	W	R	Y	U	L
H	R	N	H	R	R	P	R	Z	H	B	Y
S	E	L	T	S	O	P	A	E	S	C	J
A	D	B	Z	H	P	P	R	N	S	Y	P
Z	W	Q	S	K	O	Q	Q	Z	W	D	K
D	C	E	P	H	A	S	N	I	S	J	W

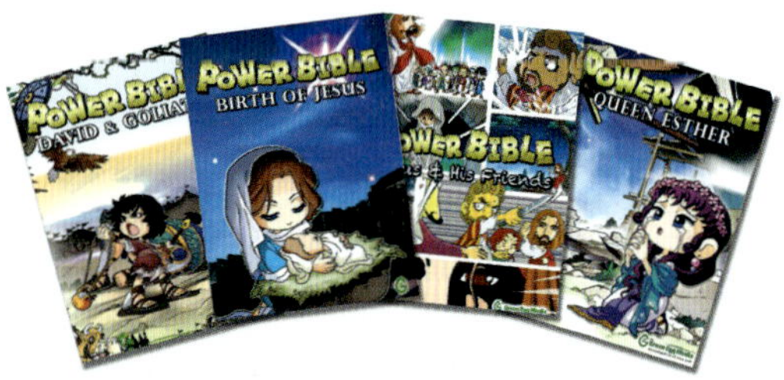

Four free comics!
Print them out! Hand them out!

COLLECT ALL 10

316PUBLISHING.COM